THE
CRISSCROSS
DOUBLE-CROSS

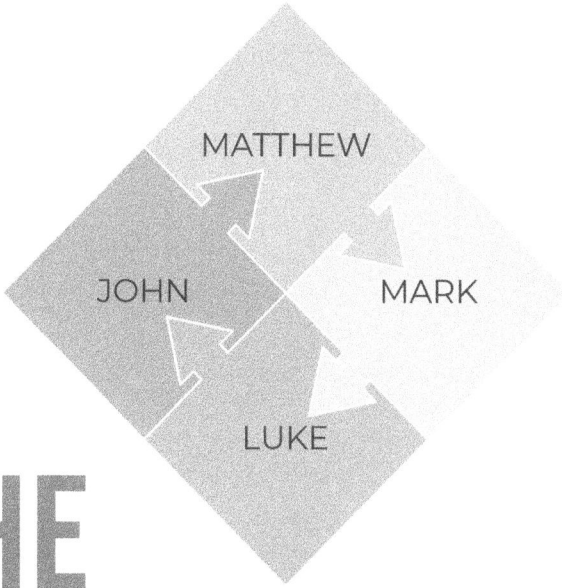

MATTHEW

JOHN

MARK

LUKE

THE
CRISSCROSS
DOUBLE-CROSS

DARWIN SATOR

LitPrime
"Your story is our priority"

LitPrime Solutions
21250 Hawthorne Blvd
Suite 500, Torrance, CA 90503
www.litprime.com
Phone: 1-800-981-9893

Published by LitPrime Solutions   03/21/2023

ISBN: 979-8-88703-178-1(sc)
ISBN: 979-8-88703-179-8(hc)
ISBN: 979-8-88703-180-4(e)

Library of Congress Control Number: 2023903430

I've written millions of words, but no books.

Since this first book may be my last, I dedicate it jointly, with love,

to Mary Kate, my wife and Florene, my mother

who deserved a lot more from me.

CONTENTS

PART 1

THE STORY

1

HERE'S THE PITCH

Then said Jesus unto him, Except ye see signs and wonders, ye will not believe.

If you are like most Christians, all of those contradictions have caused you to wonder whether there might be something wrong with the Bible. Oh boy! Were you right!

Everyone wants to know something really important, something exciting, something no one else knows. This is your chance.

After you finish this book, you'll be able to smile knowingly, if not smugly, whenever the subject of the Christian Bible comes up. You'll know more about its origins and history than will any of your friends, and you'll be able to tell them why it contains so many contradictions. Now isn't that alone worth the purchase price?

Where I grew up near Dayton, Ohio, the birthplace of Frigidaire, people had an expression for something really difficult. They'd say, "That'd be like trying to sell an icebox to an Eskimo." (Presumably, one living in an igloo.)

Our job ought to be easier than that since, for the most part, we're "preaching to the choir." But most Christians are, as they say, "up to here" in Christian theories, just as Eskimos are up to their parkas in ice.

Jesus, who knew us well, said, "Except ye see signs and wonders, ye will not believe." But like any respectable icebox salesman – against all odds – we're still going to try to make a sale. We're going to tell you that:

- Some people 1,500 years ago sabotaged the Christian Bible, and we know for certain what they did and how they did it.

- We are pretty sure who the vandals were, and exactly when, where and why they did what they did.

- We know for sure that most of the damage can be repaired!

- We think all Christians, among others, should care.

While some bits of evidence are inconclusive in themselves (it has been 1,500 years, after all) we believe you'll find the pool of evidence extremely compelling.

Because this story has a large number of facets, it is presented as a series of essays, for lack of a better term, instead of in an uninterrupted narrative. And we apologize if sometimes it is difficult to see where all the odds and ends fit together, but nothing was included willy-nilly. This approach was inspired by the idea that a person CAN eat a whole elephant – if he takes it one bite at a time.

Again with apology, since The Gospel was constructed largely of repetitive elements, a good bit of repetitious explanation also is necessary. Consolation for those who can't stand repetition – or elephant jerky – is that this is a reasonably short book.ideas on all.

2

AUTHOR'S MOTIVES

As I looked back over what I had written, I could see how some readers might suspect me of being anti-Christian.

That thought was almost enough to make me give up the whole idea. The last thing I wanted to do was to undermine another Christian's beliefs, because Jesus is also MY guiding light.

So, I decided to try to convince you – no matter what your Christian persuasion, or even non-Christian persuasion – that Jesus' words have been corrupted, and that understanding how they have been corrupted is in the interest of all of us.

I hope you'll come to see that the tares (weeds) sown among Jesus' words – which are included in our corrupted New Testament – were strewn there to mislead Jesus' followers into thinking it is not necessary to obey the Ten Commandments, or to love one's neighbor, or to respect women.

Worst of all, for 1,500 years, the tares have inspired unspeakable crimes against the Jews. To me, a child of the 20th century, the Holocaust is the only reality, and I am convinced that unless anti-Semitic forgeries in the New Testament are recognized as such, there is little chance the horror will ever end.

Still, I don't favor changing the gospels as we know them – not yet, at least, because that would be too traumatic. Our generation can live with those forgeries so long as we know they are there, and how they got there. Christians are supposedly people of good will, after all, and we can tiptoe through those noxious weeds, hopefully, until we can agree on how to exterminate them.

My purpose is to alert Christians about biblical vandalism that I believe research and future document discoveries will confirm, eventually allowing the damage to be fixed to the satisfaction of reasonable men and women. In the meantime, I'm going to tell you how it COULD be fixed, NOW.

I would hope, too, that restoring The Gospel someday will result in the founding of at least one church devoted solely to Jesus' teachings. None exists, to my knowledge.

Whatever we do, we must not wait another 1,500 years to rescue The Gospel; it might be our last chance. This is intended as a start. It's up to someone else to build on it. Someone, for example, needs to check some of the restorations in this book with computers; I'm confident their validity can be proved mathematically. Could that someone be you? Let's help to fulfill Jesus' promise that "Heaven and earth shall pass away, but my words shall not pass away."

Lastly, for any misguided person who might think it's important who I am or am not, and perhaps like to attack me personally, the following is provided.

Darwin Sator

ABOUT THE AUTHOR

The author was born Darwin Sato (cq) in Pittsburgh in 1932, son of a Japanese-American father and an American-born mother of British and German ancestry. He spent most of his childhood in the village of West Milton, Ohio, leaving in 1950 at age 17 to earn a degree in journalism from The Ohio State University.

While serving as a U.S. Air Force officer in Turkey in the 1950s, Sator became very familiar with the geography and history of the lands of the New Testament: Asia Minor, Palestine, Egypt, Greece, Rome. In the intervening years, he has been unable to shake his fascination with the Mediterranean world, particularly Asia Minor, to which he has returned many times. He probably has covered more ground there than the Apostle Paul did, albeit not all on foot.

Paul was Sator's original inspiration, and for years he followed his footsteps hither and thither, so to speak. But the more roads he traveled, the closer he came to one startling conclusion: Paul had never been there!

As an editor, Sator worked during the days of the cold war, space race and civil rights struggle. As a business writer, he interviewed the David Rockefellers, Armand Hammers and Famous Amoses and covered Fortune 500 companies, hostile takeovers, nuclear energy, labor negotiations, plant closings, the passing of the industrial age and the advent of the computer age.

In 1991, after 40 years as a newspaper editor, reporter and publisher, the author returned to West Milton – intending to disappear and never write again. He stuck to it, until now.

Today, Sator describes himself as a heretic but, hopefully, a friend of Jesus. Emphasizing "hopefully," he points out that one of the main villains in this book is Theophilus, whose Greek name means "friend of God," but who turns out to be nobody's friend – certainly not God's friend.

The author doesn't pretend to be a scholar – only a journalist who waited for years before writing this, hoping in vain that someone would beat him to it and relieve him of the responsibility. Finally, he interpreted a stroke, heart attack and cancer as signals to start writing.

Sator says that at all times he has heeded the words of the Spirit in the book of Revelation:

"If any man shall add unto these things, God shall add unto him the plagues that are written in this book. And if any man shall take away from the words of the book of this prophecy, God shall take away his part out of the book of life, and out of the holy city, and from the things which are written in this book."

3

CALL IT JOURNALISM

"He who waits to do a great deal of good at once, will never do anything"
— From a Chinese fortune cookie

Great truths are all around us, even in fortune cookies. We just have to recognize them when we find them, and act on them.

If you had a turkey, trimmings and pumpkin pie, would you postpone or call off Thanksgiving dinner because you had no cranberry sauce?

What would you do if you discovered that someone sabotaged the Bible, and you were pretty sure who did it, how they did it, why they did it, and how to fix it? Would you put off telling anyone until you were sure of every detail? For a year? For 10 years? Would you take the secret to your grave?

It would take seven lifetimes to digest all of the biblical scholarship of the last 1,500 years, let alone to do anything with it. So there was no point in waiting for perfect enlightenment. It was obvious that no other individual, or committee, was going to write this book, but it needed to be written. It'd just have to be imperfect; waiting another 1,500 years wouldn't do.

As you already know, the author considers himself neither a biblical scholar nor historian, but a journalist. A journalist's job is to dispassionately gather information from as many believable sources as he can, combine it, refine it and explain it objectively – all in as few words as possible.

So, this is not offered as biblical scholarship or history or, perish the thought, creative writing. It's offered as journalism. O.K., interpretive journalism, and sometimes we'll be using the editorial "we," as you may have noticed.

There's one thing journalists have in common with scholars, historians, doctors and auto repairmen. They make mistakes. But to paraphrase the wisdom of the fortune cookie: He who puts off a task until he's sure he's ready to do it all will never do anything.

Having said that, the first part of this book is based on research and educated guesses by two men who, working separately, spent a combined 60 years contemplating what happened with the Bible during the early years of Christianity. The guesses are cross-referenced against the King James Version – the Bible as we have received it – and against history, again as we've received it.

Sator says: "I fully realize that I'm too lightly armed to engage in an intellectual duel with even one true biblical scholar, let alone the thousands of others, past and present. When challenged, I'm likely to turn and flee.

"As you read this, however, I think you'll be surprised at some of the possibilities that those otherwise brilliant scholars missed. It is difficult to say why they missed them – only that they missed them.

"Real truth tends to be simple, so often a comparative dimwit has the edge; an apple drops onto his head, so to speak. He may not deserve the credit, but who said life is fair?

"Although this book won't pry open any closed minds, I think it contains enough evidence to convince reasonable, open-minded men and women that there is far more than guesswork involved here."

You may notice that neither the Old Testament nor the Paulist writings are examined closely here. The author contends that IT WAS NEVER INTENDED that The Gospel actually be attached to the Old Testament. The Gospel stands alone, although knowledge of the Old Testament is necessary for the full understanding of the New. For the latter reason, incidentally, it should be a little easier for a Jew to understand The Gospel than for someone actually born into the Christian fold.

Likewise, the Paulist writings never should have been appended to The Gospel, even though THAT WAS INDEED THE INTENTION of the people who corrupted The Gospel. The author says the Bible, as we have received it, is a lot like what you might get by combining a 50-year-old Cleveland telephone directory with the current Cleveland, Tel Aviv and Athens phone books. Such a "communications bible" wouldn't be very helpful.

"The *Crisscross Double-cross* started out to be a historical novel," Sator says. "First, I recognized that people's imaginations are more likely to be captured by fiction than non-fiction, as book sales and movie attendance prove. Moreover, I knew that many would justifiably doubt my credentials for writing history – let alone for "rewriting" it – and I myself questioned my ability to make bare facts sufficiently interesting. Then, on Jan. 24, 2001, that all became moot.

My computer files, including the nearly completed novel – about 10 years of work – were accidentally erased. Was that a sign?

"After months of grieving, and coming to realize that the years of lost effort couldn't be reconstructed in the time I had left, I decided to try to rescue what I could – the factual basis. The result is a much shorter work incorporating both journalism and "educated" guesses – interpretive reporting, if you will.

"Those of you who would prefer a purely historical approach should know this: History is only a time-honored amalgamation of fact, fabrication, fantasy and propaganda, and there's a good reason it's that way. A lot of gaps have to be filled in.

"Historical fiction, which is enjoying great popularity, takes it a step further, and there's far too much historical fiction and too little history, for all its shortcomings, written nowadays. So I thought the least I could do was start out trying to be faithful to history, as opposed to starting out trying to write fiction.

"Although the computer ate all of the action and dialogue, I think you'll be stunned by the remaining tale of intrigue, the real-life characters and, to my way of thinking, the ultimate romance, which is the pursuit of truth.

"This book is a labor of love even though, admittedly, it frequently has an edge to it. If someone injured my loved ones, I would want to help them recover. If someone set fire to my home I would want to rebuild it. I'm going to try to convince you that God gave us the instructions for life (The Gospel, the truth, Jesus himself), and they fell among thieves 1,500 years ago. We can ignore the bleeding victim and pass by on the other side, or we can be Good Samaritans. I'll point out who I believe the culprits were and what they did, then I'll try to show you that we can undo most of what they did.

"Some will argue that our forebears lived by The Gospel just as it is, and it served them well. They'll say if it ain't broken, don't fix it. But The Gospel IS broken, and the damage AIN'T trivial. It has been made to say many things its author didn't intend, which has led many astray, and caused them to do shameful things in the name of Jesus.

"Sadly, the evidence shows that the vandals loved neither Jesus, nor Jesus' father, the God of the Jews. They couldn't stand the thought of loving their neighbors, either, a fact that is reflected in the many changes they made in The Gospel.

"Vandalizing The Gospel also has resulted in most of Christianity (Catholic, Protestant and otherwise) becoming rooted in the teachings of the man Paul and his successors, instead of the teachings of Jesus. Whatever Paul's good points were (and he had some), he taught that we really don't need the Ten Commandments and we really don't need to do good works. He also was an anti-Semite and a misogynist (he had trouble with Jews and women).

"I would hope that, in time, I would forgive someone who killed my family or torched my home. In like manner, I finally have managed to forgive those who vandalized The Gospel; I'm not mad at anybody. I just want to resurrect Jesus' words.

"To anyone who would accuse me of arrogance or blasphemy and of trying to 'rewrite' the Bible, I offer no reply. I don't know what to say to anyone who doesn't think God's Word is important. I say only that – despite my shortcomings and any accidental traces of fiction – I composed this in the spirit of truth."

4

THE REAL HOLY LAND

The following few pages describe the setting for the birth of The Gospel and Christianity.

❧

Ask most people where Christianity began, and they'll likely say Palestine. Not so. Both the New Testament and the church were born in Asia Minor, which corresponds roughly with today's Turkey.

Someone recently wrote a novel about my hometown in Ohio, mentioning the names of dozens of landmarks and dozens of people I knew while I was growing up. When I heard about the book, I rushed out to get a copy, and enjoyed it – but not as much as I had anticipated.

It was my fault; I had forgotten that the book was fiction. Most of those familiar names from my childhood were attached to characters and places that weren't anything like their real-life counterparts. They weren't meant to be.

That isn't the best possible analogy, because I regard Jesus as real, not fictional. Certainly, the truths he taught would be real, even if it turned out that he himself were fictional. But a visit years ago to Christian sites in Palestine (Jordan then; Israel today) made me suspicious about the details. Were the people and places mentioned in The Gospel like the people and places in the book about my hometown? Were they pretty much just names to the Gospel writer?

My Holy Land visit was before much Western-style development, and there were few tourists; at least, I didn't see any. So it should have been fairly easy to visualize the area as the setting for Jesus' ministry. It seemed to me that if there was any place where I might encounter an aura, it would be the Holy Land. But no.

Maybe it was all of the churches built atop sites associated with Jesus. Bible in hand, I went from Jerusalem to Bethlehem, Hebron, Bethany, the Jordan River, Dead Sea, Nazareth, the Sea of Galilee – all familiar names learned in childhood. But as much as I tried to associate those storied names and Jesus with those places, I couldn't do so. The trail was stone cold.

I've talked to other people who have visited Palestine, and several have reported the same experience. While the author of The Gospel certainly knew his Palestinian geography, he didn't seem to know enough about any place to describe it. Why? Who knows?

To experience Christian deja vu, one needs to visit Turkey (Asia Minor), where John wrote The Gospel. Strangely, while Jesus supposedly never reached Turkey, I could "feel" his presence there, while I couldn't in Palestine.

Asia Minor was mentioned in the Old Testament – it was on Mr. Ararat that Noah's Ark landed, and it was at Harran, where man (in the person of Abraham) first heard the voice of God. But Asia Minor is also the undisputed cradle of the New Testament. First and foremost, it was at Ephesus where John wrote The Gospel, and all of the Seven Churches of Asia addressed in Revelation were in what is now western Turkey. At Antioch, followers of Jesus were first called Christians. At Tarsus was born a man named Paul, who would become the standard bearer for Christians, and Asia Minor would be his battlefield. Armenia, which occupied much of what is now eastern Turkey, was the first Christian nation.

The ecumenical councils at Nicaea, Ephesus, Chalcedon and Constantinople, all in Asia Minor, formulated the Christian doctrine that survives to this day. Those bodies decided, no less, on the very natures of God, Jesus and the Holy Ghost, and how they were related to one another. It was in Asia Minor that Jesus was deified, the Nicene Creed was formulated, the Trinity was born, and Mary was proclaimed Mother of God.

God is revealed to man in different ways, and it's not always a burning bush; sometimes it's a place. I'm reminded of Florence Nightingale, and her reaction to ancient Thebes. She wondered how people "could come back from Egypt and live lives as they did before." That was before the Crimean War, and she definitely would not live her life as before.

I, too, have seen Thebes, but it was Asia Minor or Turkey that changed MY life. There are two places in the world that no Christian should miss, and if you guess Jerusalem and Rome, you're wrong. The twin Meccas of Christianity are in Turkey. One is the ruins of the ancient city of Ephesus, which most Christians have heard of, but know nothing about, and the other is the caves of Cappadocia, of which most Christians haven't even heard.

Since it's really essential that you get a feel for what those places once were, I thought I might give you a capsule description of each from the encyclopedia. I couldn't do that, of course, and decided instead to include the following journal notes from when I first saw Ephesus and Cappadocia nearly 50 years ago.

Please excuse this verbal "slide show," but I hope you'll begin to see Asia Minor as I saw it.

5

EPHESUS

Early Christians believed the Gospel writer and the disciple were the same.

April 21, 1957 (Easter)

EPHESUS – On the way here, we stopped along the road to see a camel caravan and I snapped a picture of Mary Kate hugging a baby camel. Then, when we got to the ruins, I climbed a stack of a half-dozen column capitals and Mary Kate took my picture. The latter is not proper behavior for someone claiming to have respect for archaeology, but I figured that a thousand little boys had done it, and I couldn't add much to that damage.

It seemed strange, it being Easter morning, that we were the only two people at Ephesus. As early as the year 200, a church council convened here to discuss when Easter should be observed, and for centuries pilgrims came here at Eastertime to honor John.

As it did this year, Easter usually comes in April at the time of Passover, during the Hebrew month of Nisan. The month of April is still called Nisan by the Turks, a Muslim people.

The place ought to be crawling with tourists, but there aren't any. There isn't a soul living there, either, although the city once was home to at least a quarter-million people. But there wasn't even a squatter when we were there; just Mary Kate and me.

I climbed to the yet-unexcavated top rows of the theater, where the Bible says an ugly crowd of 35,000 turned against Paul, shouting "Great is Diana of the Ephesians." I sat down, and was treated to a panorama of the cradle of Christianity. With a purple-pink blossomed Judas tree growing wild in the foreground, the white-marble Arcadian Way stretched from the theater to the west, ending abruptly at the longsilted-up harbor. Not only John and Paul, but Antony and Cleopatra trod – or were carried along – the Arcadian Way.

Visible to the north – along the dirt road entering the ruins – were the remains of the huge Church of the Virgin Mary where the Ecumenical Council of 431 met. A pitched battle between two factions was waged in that church. The disagreement, unbelievable at that late date, was over who Jesus was. One faction held that he was more God than man; the other viewed him more as an ideal man. When the smoke cleared, Jesus emerged as God, period.

In front of me also, on the Marble Street just outside the theater, was the center of Ephesian life, the lower agora, or marketplace. Just to the left of the agora was the shell of the Library of Celsus, one of the great libraries of antiquity, and lying on the ground just beyond that, the gargantuan fluted columns of a temple dedicated to the Egyptian god Serapis.

It was easy to imagine John buying papyrus in that marketplace and visiting that library. And it was easy to imagine the proud high priest of the Temple of Serapis seeing to it that Egyptian papyrus was always available in his neighborhood market.

John's presence could be felt everywhere. From high ground we could see the island of Samos to the southwest. Patmos, where John is said to have written Revelation, lay just beyond.

After exploring the middle city, we proceeded northeast, past a great hole in the ground where once rose a temple numbered among the Seven Wonders of the World. The temple was dedicated to Artemis, the Anatolian mother goddess, who later became identified with her Roman counterpart, Diana. Diana was greatly revered in Paul's time, as he found out, but she, in turn, would be eclipsed later by Mary, mother of Jesus. Tradition says Mary accompanied John to Ephesus.

On a hill beyond the Temple of Artemis, we came to our main quest, the ruins of the Temple or Church of St. John, also called the Temple or Church of the Theotokos. Theotokos, a Greek word, roughly means the repository of God. There's little doubt that the temple once held God's Word – the original Gospel.

We found the ruins of a magnificent 6th century basilica strewn with many-colored marbles. Its architect was Isidorus of Miletus, who also built the Church of Haghia Sophia (Divine Wisdom) in Constantinople, arguably the greatest relic to survive from ancient times. The Ephesian basilica had replaced a 4th century church that was wonderful in its own right, and which itself had replaced a shrine that orginally sat atop John's tomb.

Was this greatly revered man the disciple of Jesus, or another John who authored The Gospel? Early Christians believed the Gospel writer and disciple were one and the same, and the pilgrims who thronged to Ephesus for hundreds of years after his death also believed that they were paying tribute to John the disciple AND John the Gospel author. They may have been wrong, but the Pope at the time of the Council of 431 thought they were right, too, and we have that in writing.

On Easter morning in 1957, author Darwin Sator poses along the Arcadian Way in Ephesus, while Mary Kate, traveling companion and reviewer of the author's work, strikes up a friendship. John, Paul, Antony, Cleopatra and the Great Anatolian Mother Goddess also passed this way.

We didn't find the tomb (we didn't expect to, of course) but we did find the baptismal, a walk-through affair built into the floor. Brushing dirt from the floor revealed splendid mosaics, which we quickly covered up again. Those things need to be preserved but, since Turkey is one huge open-air museum, the country can't afford to protect all of its architectural treasures, at least not as fast as they are being uncovered. Hopefully, someday tourist dollars will pay for these things.

We had to do one more thing before leaving, and that was to visit the "House of the Virgin Mary" on top of a hill called Bulbul Dagi. Although we were skeptical, the legend is very old – witness the Church of the Virgin Mary in which the council met; it was the first church ever known to be dedicated to her. The Mary legend stems from Jesus' words on the cross, when he seemed to be asking his disciple John to care for his mother.

When we reached the hilltop, we found a little stone structure built on a foundation identified as that of Mary's house. The spot had been located according to instructions of a 19th century German nun, who had a vision of it.

Even we skeptics could visualize John visiting Mary and discussing the old days, and his writing, over cups of cold water from the artesian well in front of the house. After our long day, we found drinking and washing our hands and faces in the water particularly refreshing – even spiritually refreshing. We're looking forward to seeing Cappadocia next.

6

CAPPADOCIA

Although the last Christians left years ago, their spirits linger, and their blood still courses through the veins of the local Turks.

May 26, 1957

GOREME, CAPPADOCIA – The trip was easier this time. A year ago we came by way of Aksaray, literally following a caravan trail and passing many camels and some ruined caravansaries along the way. Sometimes the wind and rain had erased even the caravan trail, and we got lost and had a tough time finding our way back to it. A couple of times we asked caravan crews how far it was to our destination, and we were told two or three days (evidently the walking time). Fortunately, it was quicker by Jeep.

This time we decided to drive from Ankara to Kayseri, a slightly more direct route to the heart of Cappadocia. What a difference! Although there still are only two fairly lengthy stretches of hard-surface road in Turkey, some gravel roads, such as the one we took yesterday, are passable year-round. Or so they say.

I can't begin to describe what we saw, but while Mary Kate and I both considered ourselves Christians before yesterday, we now agree that we didn't REALLY become Christians until we saw this place. Of all the great works of man, Cappadocia is the only one that leaves you speechless. The spirit of Jesus is palpable here, as it is in Ephesus.

Cappadocia is huge – about 60 miles square or 3,600 square miles, the size of three Rhode Islands.

Sprinkled throughout the area are thousands of what Turks call fairy chimneys – tall, weirdly shaped formations sculpted from the rock by water, wind and time. The rock is tuff, made up of compacted ash and debris spewed out by the volcano Erciyas Dagi (Argaeus in Greek) more than 30 million years ago.

That sight alone is well worth the cost of a 7,000-mile trip from Ohio, but it's only the beginning.

Chiseled out of the soft rock cones, spires and cliffs are chapels, churches and monasteries dating from the earliest days of Christianity – hundreds and hundreds of them! Sculpted from living rock are pillars, pilasters, domes, vaults, arches, transepts, apses, naves and other architectural features imitating those of free-standing buildings, these replete with kitchens, banquet tables, benches, water cisterns and wine cellars. Some even have burial chambers that were sealed with millstone-shaped rocks, perhaps like the one protecting Jesus' grave, as described in The Gospel.

Walls and ceilings of the chapels and churches are decorated with brightly painted scenes from the Bible: the Last Supper, baptism in the Jordan, turning water into wine, angels, Mary and child, all of the saints and martyrs who ever lived. Some of the paintings are very good, some crude and virtually all of them defaced, but they constitute by far the world's largest collection of Byzantine art.

There are many thousands of man-made cave homes in Cappadocia, some of them dating to Hittite times, or long before the Christian era, but also many "modern" ones incorporating features like balconies and window ledges. There is no telling when the first Christians arrived; few even try to guess because, other than the thousand-year-old paintings, there are few clues. Peter, however, supposedly wrote to the Hebrews of the Dispersion living in Cappadocia and Paul is said to have preached there. Later, dropouts from the Crusades swelled the population.

Many of the church fathers, who would make their reputations in Antioch, Alexandria, Constantinople and Rome, were born here or lived here at one time or another. Basil the Great (329-379), bishop of Caesarea (the afore-mentioned Kayseri), was instrumental in establishing monastic communities in Cappadocia that lasted a thousand years. Here, Gregory the Theologian (c. 325-390) created the liturgy that became the Gregorian chant.

Mary Kate and I spent the night in a village called Ortahisar, which was built around a central rock column that I would guess is 20 storeys high, hollowed out and inhabited from bottom to top. The nearby ground-level "hotel" in which we stayed harbored some fleas, but also a rooster, which saw that we got an early start after a breakfast of white cheese, ekmek (bread), rose-petal jam and tea.

There is fruit of all kinds here, especially many varieties of apricots, since this is where they first were cultivated. The Roman general Lucullus took home both apricots and cherries, which he found growing just to the north of here; they were unknown in Europe. The early Christians must have made great wine.

As at Ephesus, no protection is provided for this world archaeological site. There are no tourists, but families (and their animals) still live in many of the rock dwellings, including the former churches and chapels, blackening muraled walls with their cooking fires.

We saw an example of "spring cleaning," which is accomplished by chiseling the grimy surfaces off of the soft rock walls and ceilings – a messy but fairly easy task. That leaves an agreeable light, sandy surface and, repeated many times, produces a bonus: a significantly enlarged home. Unfortunately, sometimes it also removes the Byzantine "wallpaper" (frescoes).

We found a single caretaker in Cappadocia, who was living in the valley at Goreme, the most interesting of several valleys and troglodyte villages we had time to sample. The eyes of the pious old man lit up as he talked about his beloved valley. After pouring tea for us, he recalled that when he was a boy he saw an "underground city" where "a hundred thousand" Christians hid during tough times. I suspect that was a fantasy, although he seemed knowledgeable, mentioning Persians, Tamerlane and marauding Arabs among the pursuers.

Fantasy or not, this place nevertheless provided refuge for Christians over many, many centuries. And although the last Christians left a few years ago, their spirits linger, and their blood still courses through the veins of the local Turks.

October 20, 2002

Seeing Cappadocia is like staring into Olduvai Gorge, where some of our earliest ancestors were born, or peering through a telescope at the Eagle Nebula, and seeing the light from stars being born 7,000 years ago. Forget the books. There is instant, instinctual recognition at the first sight of Cappadocia. This is the birthplace of Christianity. The details are lost in time, but the sight of Cappadocia leaves little doubt in the mind of the first-time visitor, who is stunned to near silence.

Many other awe-inspiring spots, among them Auschwitz-Birkenau, Hiroshima and Stalingrad (Volgograd), have to do with death. Cappadocia is about life.

Cappadocia is where The Gospel set off a chain reaction that changed the world. All of the great truths are not written down in books, because man's lifetime is short, his memory is short, his imagination is limited and his head is full of nonsense. Man makes up myths and religions to explain what he doesn't know, and he really missed on this one.

Forty-five years after my first visits, I am pleased to note that the Turkish government has taken many steps to preserve both Ephesus and Cappadocia, and both have become world tourist attractions, which, of course, is good and bad, but it's mostly good. And the old caretaker's "underground city" was no fantasy. In fact, several underground cities have been found, cut out of rock to a depth of seven storeys or more and large enough to hold many thousands of Christians.

Cappadocia holds more secrets. Maybe even a scroll or two.

This hollowed-out rock of about 20 storeys is in a town
in Cappadocia. Thousands were made into churches,
chapels and dwellings in the early years of Christianity.

7

'INDIANA JONES'

They would not listen, they did not know how

Two thousand years ago, Jesus walked among us, sowing seeds of wisdom. But in the end, when not even his disciples fully understood what he was talking about, he said he'd send another Comforter to guide us – to explain everything we needed to know – presumably when we were ready and able to listen.

That Comforter, obviously, was John, who gave the world The Gospel. But, as Jesus said, "Give not that which is holy unto the dogs, neither cast ye your pearls before swine, lest they trample them under their feet, and turn again and rend you." The Gospel certainly was trampled and torn apart.

If life were like Hollywood – if life were fair – the original, unspoiled Gospel of Jesus, or a copy of the same, would turn up in a cave in Cappadocia or at Ephesus, as the Dead Sea Scrolls did in Palestine, or the Gnostic writings did in Egypt. Just imagine…

Some of us have fantasized about finding the Holy Grail or the Ark of the Covenant, which contained the tables inscribed with the

Ten Commandments that Moses brought down from Mt. Sinai. Those fantasies became movie plots.

To this day, every synagogue has its own ark, but since Moses didn't make enough tablets to go around, instead of tablets, present-day arks contain the Torah on parchment scrolls. Torah is the name for the first five books of the Old Testament, the most revered books of the Hebrew Bible.

I want to tell you about a real-life "Indiana Jones." He was an American who died in 1989, leaving us a veritable Christian torah, a scroll inscribed with the first four books of the New Testament – the heart and soul of the Christian Bible. In a very real sense The Gospel, too, had been lost, because it had been 1,500 years since it was last seen intact.

The man who rediscovered the original Gospel wasn't an archaeologist, and he didn't find scrolls in some cave. He worked 30 years figuring out the patterns the author used to create The Gospel in the first place, and how to use them to reconstruct the manuscript. His accomplishment was extraordinary. It was much like another popular fantasy: re-creating a long-extinct animal from DNA recovered from permafrost or amber. A movie was made of that one, too.

The world ignored our hero. It would not listen; it did not know how. Didn't Jesus say, "A prophet is not without honor, except in his own country"?

Twenty-five silent years have passed.

8

THE ILLUMINATOR

We can't keep calling the man who saved The Gospel Indiana Jones, but we're still not quite ready to identify him. (We're trying to weave a mystery here, after all.) So, for now, we're going to call him The Illuminator, which has a history in the church, and which we think is appropriate for someone who shed fresh light on the Bible.

The Illuminator first started thinking about the Bible in unconventional terms at age 37, while teaching a class at his church.

A note found after his death said: "To my overwhelming surprise, not to say consternation (as well as that of my wife), the more I studied the Bible, the deeper I became in completely revolutionizing my my ideas on all subjects having to do with myself as an individual and the relations of human beings to each other and to the world in general. (It) has completely changed my life, to my great joy."

A few years later he started making notes in spiral notebooks – the first entries in pencil. While faint and difficult to read, penciled notes had the advantage of being erasable, and notebooks full of erasures, line-outs and scribbled changes multiplied.

Astoundingly, The Illuminator managed to piece together most of his theories with little more help than the *Encyclopaedia Britannica* and a couple of beat-up, old reference books: an 1881 edition of Westscott and Hort's *New Testament in Greek* and a 1936 edition of Funk and Wagnalls' *New Standard Bible Dictionary.*

He quickly saw it would be impossible to re-create, with only a lead pencil, a scroll like the original, which likely was produced by a professional scribe. (He was convinced the original was a single scroll). The breakthrough came when one day he spotted some very inexpensive Bibles for sale at a local 5-and-10-cent store. He bought one of the Bibles, purchased a roll of wide butcher paper, then started cutting up the pages of the book and pasting chapters and verses where he guessed they belonged on the original scroll. He needed two Bibles at a time, because the leaves were printed on both sides, and the cutting rendered every other page unusable.

Destroying Bibles wasn't easy for our hero, as he loved the book, and some pious friends were aghast at such apparent vandalism. (We were a lot more sensitive in those days.)

Fortuitously, the dime-store Bible was a red-letter edition, with all of Jesus' words in red ink. That proved to be a help initially in spotting places where vandalism might have occurred. The Illuminator bought the rest of the store's stock, and he'd buy many more Bibles over the next 25 years.

The first Bible scraps were affixed to the scroll with mucilage, but that proved to be a problem because, invariably, the first placement would not be exactly right, and the flimsy paper couldn't be removed without tearing. After much frustration, dabs of rubber cement were substituted, allowing a verse to be taken from one place and moved to another, sometimes several times. Ironically, the process of restoring The Gospel was a lot like the ancients used in vandalizing it.

Years later, as the restored document approached its final form, a secretary typed copies with an extra-large typewriter. Wood racks, each about 5 feet high with two spindles, made it possible to view large sections of the scroll at one time.

The mechanics, however, were a relatively minor problem.

Inspiration came slowly, spread out over 30 years.

When asked how he could discover what others hadn't seen in 1,500 years, our hero would say: "For about the first thousand of those years, printing had not been invented, and copies of the scriptures were not available to most people… not until the King James Version came along in 1611." When asked why someone hadn't seen these things SINCE 1611, he would reply: "Partly because no one has been willing to put in 30 years' study of them, and partly because powers of perception vary in different people."

Never was anything more true than the latter. Scientists have confirmed that there are a few people who can't tell colors apart, taste food, smell a skunk, or recognize the Star-Spangled Banner until people around them rise to their feet. People who lack those senses probably shouldn't try to become painters, chefs, perfume makers or orchestra directors.

There are some people, on the other hand, who have amazingly keen senses. The Illuminator, for example, took one look at the vandalized Gospel and recognized it as just one huge crossword puzzle. He explained the process of solving it:

"From some of the pieces which were not broken apart (the puzzle solver) learns the system, pattern or architect's plans by which the autograph (a manuscript in an author's handwriting) was written. Then, with the aid of that knowledge, he puts part of the pieces together here, and part of the pieces together there. Then he finds that the first group of pieces assembled together fit like a jigsaw puzzle into the other assembled groups of pieces, and these, in turn, fit into the parts of the manuscript which were never cut apart, and which lay scattered about or jumbled together." Easy for him; impossible for the rest of us!

The Illuminator wasn't a particularly humble man. He was, in fact, proud of his deductive reasoning ability and, after being asked about how he could know so much, he often told one of his famous stories about how Sherlock Holmes solved a crime. Ultimately, however, he learned that even a Sherlock Holmes had to learn humility. He would recall being brought so low that he had to beg God for each tiny shred of inspiration – for permission to go on.

By the time you finish *The Crisscross Double-cross,* you SHOULD want to know more about the man and, by then, maybe you'll DESERVE to know more. So, a short biography on Page 362 will at least put a face on him.

But wait! Don't look yet! The first thing we'll do here is try to reconstruct the extraordinary chain of events leading up to, and including, the rape of The Gospel. That story is Part 1. Part 2 is an explanation of the techniques used in restoring The Gospel. Part 3 consists of restorations extrapolated from the Illuminator's handwritten notes, which are in the possession of the writer of this book.

9

SEPPHORIS, JESUS' CITY

*God is love. God is a spirit. Jesus is truth. Jesus is the
Son of God. Are the details important?*

If, as we have said, it is so difficult for some to "find" Jesus in the
Holy Land, shouldn't we be asking ourselves whether The Gospel
of Jesus might not be fiction?

Some people say they can't accept the teachings of Jesus because
his contemporaries didn't mention him, and because the Bible is his
only witness. That's understandable, but it is a mistake, since Jesus'
teachings speak for themselves and, at the same time, testify to the
existence of God.

Accordingly, the better part of 2 billion people consider Jesus to
be God's Word to the world, and many consider The Gospel the most
perfect distillation of the truth ever uttered. But those who insist that
every word of the New Testament be taken literally are making a
mistake, too. A big mistake.

To begin with, most of the Bible is allegorical – like the Old
Testament's Noah and the Ark and Jonah in the whale – and

EVERYTHING Jesus said was allegorical. We know the latter because The Gospel tells us that Jesus "taught them in parables and without a parable he taught them not." Jesus didn't intend for us to take his parables literally; he used them to illustrate truths – all of the time. The word parable appears 48 times in The Gospel.

According to The Gospel, Jesus lived in Galilee during the reign of Tiberius. But is The Gospel a literally true biography? Is its setting in Galilee essential geography? Is its association with Tiberius essential history?

How you feel about the details may depend a lot on whether or not you think Jesus needs to be authenticated as a historical figure. But is historicity important to Jesus' message? Think how many, many more details of his life and ministry are missing? Should we be concerned about them?

When the Gospel writer was, let's say, commissioned by God to give us the story of Jesus, the writer didn't sweat the small stuff. He didn't tell us one-tenth of 1 percent of what happened in Jesus' life, and he told us even less about the world in which Jesus lived. You'll see later why this is an important point, but first let's look at one example of what we're talking about.

Have you ever heard of Sepphoris? Most people haven't. Yet Sepphoris was a metropolis – the capital of Galilee, a regional political and administrative center until Jesus was in his early twenties – and it was only 4 miles north of Nazareth, the town where he grew up!

Since Sepphoris would be only an hour's walk from Nazareth, it is certain that Jesus spent much time there. He almost certainly ran errands there as a boy, had friends and relatives living there, and plied his carpentry trade there. To reach Cana, only 9 miles from Nazareth, where he turned wine into water and where he healed the son of a nobleman, Jesus had to pass through Sepphoris. Yet, the city isn't even mentioned in the New Testament.

Thanks to archaeology, we now know that Sepphoris was a cosmopolitan city inhabited by Jews, Romans, Greeks and Arabs. It had paved streets flanked by colonnades, multistory buildings and major waterworks. Yet, the place isn't even mentioned in The Gospel although, again, it was only 4 miles from Nazareth.

When asked where he is from, any modern-day small towner will answer that he's from near such-and-such a city. Rural people look to big cities for identity, for excitement, for style and, unless there's a family farm and one is the eldest son, for employment possibilities. Nazarene fishermen and farmers went into Sepphoris regularly to sell their catch and crops; the women, to buy food and clothing.

Jesus didn't just fall off a turnip wagon; he was a suburbanite. Jesus' big city was Sepphoris, which was capital of Galilee until about the year 20, when Herod Antipas built Tiberias and moved there. Today, in the ruins of once cosmopolitan Sepphoris, are found mosaic and stone inscriptions in Greek, Latin, Hebrew, Aramaic and Syriac.

Also, we now know that the Mishnah, the body of law on which the Talmud is based, was codified in Sepphoris around the year 210. (Both learning and teaching, by the way, were called mishnah, meaning repetition, which is The Gospel's method.) So it is clear that Sepphoris was an important center of Hebrew erudition, meaning that Jesus no doubt received much of his education there. Likely, John did, as well. Again, 4 miles from Nazareth, but the Bible is silent.

Jesus undoubtedly came to understand and speak at least some of the languages spoken in the city in his time, surely the dominant Greek (even the Roman soldiers stationed there spoke Greek). That isn't mentioned in the Bible, either, nor is it fully appreciated by some scholars.

What does all of this prove? It proves that geography, history and even the details of Jesus' personal life weren't major concerns of the Gospel writer. So we shouldn't sweat the small stuff, either. The Gospel writer used what today we call the KISS method (Keep It Simple, Stupid). After all, it's the message of truth that counts, isn't it? And the more uncomplicated, uncluttered and unvarnished the better, wouldn't you agree? Or are you one of those Bible lawyers?

10

JESUS WAS NO CHRISTIAN

Jesus was a Jew. He added "Love thy neighbor" to the Ten Commandments.

One dictionary definition of gospel is "something, such as an idea or principle, accepted as unquestionably true."

The Gospel of Jesus, as befitting its name, is accepted by most Christians as gospel, or unquestionably true. But you don't have to live long in this world to see that man corrupts everything he touches, and he corrupted The Gospel. As a result, truth has suffered greatly.

Some may say that this kind of thinking is anti-Christian, but at least judge for yourself before casting stones. Hopefully, you will see that no one seeks to harm anyone, or to turn anyone from Christianity, or to convert anyone to some "new" Christianity. Instead, it is hoped that you will see the need to convince a few reasonable men and women of today, first, that someone corrupted the Gospel and, second, that it can be fixed, so that the unadulterated Word can be passed to the next generation, and the next.

Lastly, while perhaps there is no rush after 2,000 years, maybe you'll come to agree that the long-term future of Christianity is at stake. This is not intended to be a Christian dissertation, or a religious discourse of any kind, except it does presume the existence of God. Of course, if religion is defined by a belief in God, then nearly everybody could be said to be "religious," since most people profess belief in a higher power or intelligence – in other words, God. But deism isn't religion in the usual sense. Religion is a way of looking at deity, and it comes in various flavors, such as Christian, Hindu, Hebrew, Muslim or Buddhist. Usually, they are rigid ways of looking at diety, and we're not interested in that.

After 70 years of sampling many flavors, waiting for God to whisper the ultimate truth in his ear, the author decided that everything could be boiled down to Love your neighbor!

That brings up the author's two fondest wishes. The first is for Christians to stop hating, persecuting and killing Jews just because they are Jews. The second is for the establishment of at least one Christian church based on Jesus' teachings, whose members won't have to be embarrassed to admit being Christian.

To state what ought to be obvious, Jesus was no Christian; Jesus was a Jew, and the Old Testament was his heritage. At John IV, Verse 22, he says: "Ye worship ye know not what: we know what we worship: for salvation is of the Jews. Notice the pronoun "we."

Jesus gave us grace and truth, added "Love one another" to the Ten Commandments and preached doing good works. Yet, the church fathers felt it necessary to turn early Christians against Jesus' own people and the Hebrew religion. Again, Jesus was no Christian, and there is no evidence that he intended to spark a new religion.

Anti-Semitism has always been with us. In the year 1096, for example, Christian Crusaders massacred Jews as a warmup, or target practice, on their way to kill other Jews (and Muslims) in the Holy Land. They slaughtered the Jews of Xanten, Wevelinghofen, Neuss, Cologne, Eller, Trier, Metz, Mainz, Worms, Speyer, Ratisbon, Prague and elsewhere, in the belief that God would be pleased and that their own sins would be purged.

St. Ambrose (c. 339-397), considered one of the four greatest Latin fathers of the church, advocated burning synagogues so "that there might not be a place where Christ is denied." He characterized a synagogue as "a haunt of infidels, a home of the impious, a hiding place for madmen, under the damnation of God himself."

For 300 years, until 1870, the popes in Rome maintained their own Jewish ghetto, a miserable human zoo at the foot of Vatican Hill. An enduring symbol of Christ's supposed victory over the Jews, its impoverished residents were compelled to listen to endless sermons designed to convert them to Christianity, and to suffer the kidnapping and forced baptism of their children.

The Italian army finally freed the pope's prisoners, but not until 1870, less than 70 years before the Nazis came to power. So there actually were people living during World War II who remembered the Vatican ghetto.

For 1,500 years, Christian churches have initiated or participated in such atrocities or turned their backs as others burned synagogues, deprived Jews of their property and livelihoods, compelled them to wear identifying clothing and to work in inferior jobs, forcibly converted them to Christianity, and ghettoized, exiled, tortured and murdered them. Like it or not, the New Testament provided inspiration for all of those shameful acts.

And the Christian clergy played a disgraceful role. Protestant reformer Martin Luther called for burning the homes, schools and synagogues of Jews and driving them, "like mad dogs, out of the land."

As for the 20th century Holocaust, history assigns the blame to "the Nazis," a name that masks their true identity. When we talk about World War II, we refer to "the Japs," an opprobious epithet that, nevertheless, identifies an enemy. But we are more sensitive when it comes to the Germans. We usually say their crimes were committed by "the Nazis" or "Hitler," not by Germans.

We take it easy on the Germans because they ostensibly are Christian and Caucasian – like most of the rest of us. German troops, who wore the slogan "Gott Mit Uns" (God Is With Us) on their uniforms, didn't just enjoy the support of millions of other Germans, they also had the sympathy of millions more across Europe and millions of their American

THE CRISSCROSS DOUBLE-CROSS

cousins, most of them professed Christians. And if their churches and governments really disapproved of their crimes, they didn't show it in a big way.

It is a mistake to blame the churches entirely for the slaughter of 6 million Jews, but their ambivalence, at best, toward the Jews showed the German sadists and perverts that there wouldn't be any serious opposition anywhere. Hitler recognized that fact at the very beginning of the war, when he remarked that, already, no one remembered the massacre of the Armenians, which had happened only 20 years before.

Anti-Semitism may be "out of style today" but it's just that – out of style. Like Pasteurella pestis, the bubonic plague virus, it is only slumbering and will resurface. It always does.

It is fair, at this point, to question why we should be concerned only about the welfare of the Jews, since there also have been Christian atrocities against Muslims and other religious groups, and Muslim atrocities against both Jews and Christians. Granted, but that's another book, or books. What sets the crimes against Jews apart from the rest, other than their sheer scale, is that they have been inspired by the very words of the Christian Bible, the New Testament.

Some of us have discussions with fundamentalist Christian friends about what the Bible says or doesn't say, and they inevitably end up playing their trump card, which reads: "The Bible does not lie." Many of us quit at that point, because it turns our stomachs to have to argue that the Bible DOES, IN FACT, LIE.

Yes, the Christian Bible lies. It told the truth in the beginning and, for the most part, it still does. But 1,500 years ago a handful of churchmen (it was an inside job) vandalized The Gospel. Having little regard for Jesus, and none for his "second commandment," to love one another, they took The Gospel, scrambled its parts and added bogus material to suit themselves. In so doing, they destroyed, obscured or watered down portions of The Gospel that they didn't like and, in some cases, actually managed to turn Jesus' words against himself and against his own people.

By sowing tares, or weeds, among the words of God (see the parable of the tares), the clergy stirred up resentment and hatred toward Jews.

They also made changes to accomplish various other purposes, a few of which were aggrandizing the clergy, manufacturing an apostolic hierarchy for the church, justifying their prejudice against women, endorsing accumulation of wealth, and sanctioning slavery.

Since today's Christian clergy owe their exalted status to those vandalized scriptures, it shouldn't be surprising that they tend to rationalize the hate and prejudices of those wicked church fathers.

Again. it's not totally the fault of today's church leaders, since they do what their predecessors always have done, which is to march in unconscious lockstep (blind faith). They don't fully realize what happened, either.

In summation, somebody did something very wrong to the Christian Bible or New Testament, making it – in the corrupted condition we have received it – arguably only marginally worth saving.

11

PITY THE IK

"I am come in another's name and ye receive me not. If another shall come in his own name, him ye will receive."

—Jesus, foretelling Paul

Is the Christian Bible worth saving? All things considered, the answer has to be yes. Without it, 2 billion people would be poorer indeed. They could end up like the Ik.

Consider the Ik. The Ik are members of a formerly nomadic tribe in central Africa who are said to relish the misfortune of others.

Anthropologist Colin Turnbull, who studied the Ik and published his findings in 1972, related how they tossed their children out of the home at the age of 3. They never helped one another, and when the male hunters killed game, they ate it where they killed it, not taking it home and sharing it with the women, children, the aged and the weak.

According to Turnbull, the Ik obviously were amused by the misfortunes of others – even by their deaths, dumping the bodies of the dead unceremoniously. He said honesty among the Ik came to be regarded as foolishness, and cattle rustling became their main pursuit.

Sociologists suspect that the reason behind the Iks' icky behavior was that at the end of World War II the government of Uganda appropriated the tribe's hunting grounds for a national park and resettled them in the inhospitable mountains nearby. Lost along with the Iks' land was their culture, including social morality, which had been based on a nomadic hunting lifestyle.

Unfortunately, Turnbull died in 1994, and there has been little followup study, but the Iks of his time teach a lesson. The glue that holds together a society doesn't even have to be a formal religion; with the Iks, it was their nomadic hunting style. For much of the world, however, the glue is organized religion. So, by virtue of the fact that the lifestyles and social institutions of about 2 billion people are based to one degree or another on New Testament values, it is very important that the book eventually be repaired, not discarded.

True, the majority of the world's people aren't Christians, and most don't appear to be particularly inferior, morally, to Christians. Some appear to be superior. A few places in the world, for example, have virtually no serious crime, and the strong take better care of the young, old, weak and sick. How their people behave depends on their own (non-Christian) traditions, written and unwritten.

American and European societies, however, are based on the Christian tradition and that's unlikely to change soon. So it's important to protect the book on which their religion is based.

Another reason it's important that the book be cleaned up is so that Christians can claim the high ground. Today, another of the world's major religions, Islam, is in danger of being taken over by some of the same sort of evil forces that misused Christianity in the past and are now staging a comeback in the churches.

In either case, people aren't born hating their fellow man; much of the hate comes as a result of the Bible and the Koran being perverted and misinterpreted. Christians of goodwill and Muslims of goodwill should want to fix any offending scriptures, to the extent that they can; re-interpret them, to the extent that they can; or where they can do neither, just trash any obviously false teachings.

How do we know which teachings are false? God gave us brains and souls, and we are certain of one thing: Allah, or God, doesn't want us hating and killing one another, so no scripture that seems to tell us to hate and kill could possibly be sacred to God, or Allah.

So, for our part, we definitely DO need to clean up the Christian Bible, if we can. It is especially important because some people take every word literally, and some of those words are the words of the evil men who vandalized the Bible more than 1,500 years ago.

The Gospel, of course, was written to be understood both literally and figuratively. We know that because it tells us that Jesus spoke only in parables. Nevertheless, there always will be fundamentalists. The good news is that literal translation doesn't damage Jesus' message – quite the contrary. Literal translation helps to preserve Jesus' message, much like strict interpretation of the U.S. Constitution by the Supreme Court helps to keep American ideals from being trashed. The fundamentalists, like the Supreme Court, are needed.

However, certain evidence that The Gospel wasn't meant to be taken ONLY literally is the use of the word "parable" in the scriptures. That word occurs 48 times in The Gospel, which is about Jesus, but only 2 times in all of the rest of the New Testament – those parts having to do with Paul and the rest. So while Jesus spoke ONLY in parables and, therefore, what he said in The Gospel wasn't meant to be taken merely literally, the rest of the New Testament WAS meant to be taken literally.

But the rest of the New Testament is about Paul, the usurper, not about Jesus. Jesus foretold of Paul when he said: "I have come in another's name and ye receive me not. If another shall come in his own name, him ye will receive."

The trouble comes when the Paulist fundamentalists wind up being the only people who talk about The Gospel and the New Testament – and they talk about them only in fundamentalist terms. That causes some mainstream Christians to be embarrassed even to admit being Christian.

That also causes some to doubt their own faith. Embarrassed and confused, many people reared in "Christian homes," who would have been active Christians in another time, have quit reading the Bible and avoid churches. And, more and more, mainstream ministers simply avoid Jesus – whose name has become associated with high-pitched fanaticism and "Honk If You Love Jesus" car-bumper stickers.

But compare the Gospel-illiterate mainstream congregations with those of the fundamentalist churches, in which many rank-and-file members can quote more scripture than many of the ministers of the other churches. Which do you think will represent Christianity in the future?

12

GOD GAVE US BRAINS

"The way to see by faith is to shut the eye of reason"
—Benjamin Franklin

G ospel means the Good News. The good news (lower case) offered
here is that all parts of the New Testament that foster hate, cater
to prejudices, further selfish goals or merely cause confusion can be
identified and eliminated. They can be eliminated even though 1,500
years have passed since the vandalism that created them occurred.

Unbelievable? Stick with this.

Sadly, like the vandals who sought to improve on The Gospel, many
of today's Christians don't feel that Jesus' teachings are sufficient unto
themselves. Some even regard Jesus' teachings as simplistic. People
always have preferred complex, convoluted theologies tinged with
magic, and Christian theologians have always happily filled that need,
denying Jesus' human side and turning his message from God into a
series of mere miracles.

Down deep, however, we all know that the great truths are simple,
not complex, and Jesus spoke the simple truth. He told us that even a
child, especially a child, and maybe only a child at heart, can approach

God. In Matthew, Jesus says: "Except ye be converted, and become as little children, ye shall not enter into the kingdom of heaven." It is difficult to see any ambiguity in that.

The trouble is that we don't use our own God-given intellect – that which separates us from all of God's other creatures. The emphasis is on God-given. We look for others – disciples, apostles, popes, bishops, priests, pastors, preachers, ministers, both living and dead – to explain the words of Jesus and to intercede for us. But if we can read and pray, why should we need help from anyone, any more than we would need help in interpreting and using Dr. Benjamin Spock's classic about rearing children?

The clergy doesn't have any resources the rest of us don't have but, like lawyers, they have a vested interest in keeping things complex, and even hidden. This is not a big knock against them, because obfuscation always has gone with the territory – their territory.

To protect their territory, churches in the past have discouraged reading of the scriptures, and some still do. It's a transparent ploy. Five hundred years ago the humanist and scholar Erasmus declared:

"I fiercely oppose those people who do not want Holy Writ translated into a vernacular to be read by nonspecialists; whether Christ's teaching were so involved as to be understood by very few theologians only, or the Christian religion could be protected only if it be ignored."

At bottom, people are afraid of what they don't know, especially about death. The truth is that nobody knows more than you do. Does that frighten you a little? Of course. About 8 billion other people are a little scared, too; we're all in the same boat.

But when you consider how very little humans know about ANYTHING (Thomas Edison said, "We do not know one millionth of one percent about anything"), why is it so hard to admit we don't know about death? It's fear, and that's when the clergy – people just like us – come along with a lot of hocus-pocus and guarantee that we'll go someplace nice, if...

They teach blind faith, which means we still won't understand, but we can relax; somebody will be thinking for us. Jesus, on the other hand, taught faith in God, not in human beings – not in the clergy.

He said, "How can ye believe, which receive honour one of another and seek not the honour that cometh from God only?"

Jesus said no one had ever seen God, and that shouldn't concern anyone. He taught that anyone who wants to go to heaven should love God and his neighbor, and do good works. Jesus, too, performed some magic, but only to illustrate his teachings. Unfortunately, that caused many to believe the magic WAS his teaching, and have sought to emulate his magic.

Some ministers and priests go so far as to discourage even rational thought, advocating lives guided by faith alone. Jesus, however, tried to tell us that neither those who would place themselves above us, nor those whom we would place on thrones or pedestals are worthy of blind faith. There is no race or class of super humans that owns the ultimate truth, so why should we trust the thoughts of others rather than our own?

Placing blind faith in men may be O.K. for children but, even then, society must make laws to protect the children. Then, when an adult takes advantage of a child, that adult risks imprisonment. It is unlawful, too, to take advantage of an adult whose mind hasn't developed normally. To the vast majority of people, however, God gave minds capable of determining right and wrong. And in America, at least, there still are no laws against thinking. Not yet, anyway.

For priests and ministers to preach blind faith to adults is to take away God's greatest gift to them and, in essence, take criminal advantage. If you've chosen blind faith in men over faith in God, then we're not on the same page. Just close your eyes and put your hands over your ears.

But why not listen? You shouldn't be struck dead for listening and, as with the Bible, you won't need any help reading this short book. If you don't like it, just burn it; Christians have been burning books for 1,500 years. But at least you will have opened your mind a crack.

13

IN DOUBT? WWJD?

Zizanion is a tare – a weed with poisonous seeds resembling wheat. It is separated from the grain just before harvest.

Something happened between alpha and omega. Alpha and omega, the beginning and the end of God's Word (Jesus), became A to Z, alpha to zizanion, the beginning of the Word to its strangulation by tares. Somebody sowed weeds among the words of God.

Shortly, we will give you an idea of who sowed the tares, why they did it, and how. If you're a Christian, you should be intrigued at first, then angry. You ought to become angry when you realize that some evildoers took away your most powerful argument for being a Christian, which is: "The Bible doesn't lie."

Admittedly, the author of the book you are holding was looking for something wrong. He long had been disturbed that the Christian Bible, known as the New Testament, had been used to justify a panoply of wrongs by no means limited to the Crusades, the Inquisition, anti-Semitism, the Holocaust, colonialism, slavery, and the burning of "witches" and books. He was put off, too, by the New Testament's aggrandizement of the clergy, its baffling bias against women, and contradictions that are an insult to any thinking person. Something was seriously wrong!

But how can we assume that just because the Bible doesn't say what we would want it to say, that it doesn't say what the author intended for it to say? Isn't that a big jump? Of course, but let's apply fad philosophy by asking, What Would Jesus Do? (WWJD?).

Would Jesus hate Jews? Would he advocate persecuting and killing people just because they are Jews? Again, Jesus was a Jew, not a Christian. Jesus never heard of Christians; they hadn't been invented.

Would Jesus have contempt for women? Hardly; he surrounded himself with women. At last count, half the people in the world were women. Would Jesus choose a man he called Satan (Peter) to head his church? Hardly. And so forth, and so on. Something is very wrong.

Where do we start? How about starting this way: "In the beginning was the Word, and the Word was with God…" Ironically, it is at this very point that the forgers started to tamper with The Gospel, as we shall see.

It would be a mistake to judge the vandals, since Jesus warned against judging our fellow man, but he didn't say we couldn't judge their evil deeds and try to reverse them.

It can be demonstrated that The Gospel we know is still largely as written, at least as a percentage of the whole. A handful of men altered the rest with forgeries and other tricks of obfuscation. Collateral damage was caused by the thousands of writers who, in the intervening centuries, have unwittingly ratified the vandals' work.

Although most of those thousands have been well-meaning, most also made the mistake of assuming that the Bible, as it was handed to them, didn't lie. We make the same mistake today. Over the course of 1,500 years, in attempting to explain the unexplainable, Christians have built a mountain of myth that has both covered the vandals' tracks and further blurred the meaning of scripture.

The unchallenged myth has had at least two lasting effects. First, it has allowed latter-day evildoers to use the Bible to justify crimes against humanity; and second, it has caused Christianity to be exposed to ridicule.

That mountain of disinformation is too large for one person, or a hundred persons, to budge. In order to reach the truth, we are going to have to tunnel into that mountain. We are going to have to make some educated guesses about where the truth lay inside that mountain, so that we don't miss it with our tunneling.

Many people always will believe that the New Testament, exactly as we have received it, is the unsullied word of God. They will trust the authorities who have told them so, because they erroneously think Jesus wanted us to trust those placed above us (he didn't; Paul did). Many will continue to answer all challenges with "The Bible doesn't lie," and they are not to be blamed, because their misplaced faith leaves no room for doubt.

For everyone else, there's this advice: For the same reason you shouldn't blindly believe every automobile, insurance or snake-oil salesman, you shouldn't put BLIND faith in any religion salesman.

When you listen to a priest or a minister, you are NOT listening to God. You are listening to a man – a salesman, at that – and you should judge what he says on its merits – using the intellect God gave you. Why would God give you a brain and not want you to use it?

Religions often start out on the right foot, then men start adding to them. It follows, therefore, that whatever men add, they can subtract. In many cases, they have an OBLIGATION to subtract what they've added.

Here's a small example: Jesus himself said nothing about a celibate priesthood. So, if a celibate priesthood turns out to be a problem, why not get rid of it? And here are a couple of huge examples: It wasn't Jesus who wanted to kill Jews and to enslave the dark-skinned peoples of the world, so why go on pretending that he would sanction it? Mohammed didn't say anything about stoning women to death and flying airplanes into tall buildings, either, so why pretend that he would bless such actions?

Christian Crusades and Muslim Jihads? The same. Clerics naturally fear that admitting error might hurt their religions, but how can ceasing to do evil hurt any religion worthy of the name? Men turn religions into curses. God/Allah gave us minds and souls so that we can overcome meanness, not invent new meanness.

Blind faith in men is a real problem here, because some men long ago perverted The Gospel, in effect kidnapping Jesus and even putting lies into his mouth. They should not be allowed to get away with it – not if we can stop them. And those who have been misled into believing that "The Bible doesn't lie" should be leading an angry charge. No, that's not Christian. Let's make that a fervent charge.

14

FINDING JOHN, HUNTING PAUL

...no fragment of any of Paul's works can be dated much before the 3rd century. And we are supposed to believe that his works pre-date John's Gospel.

This story must be told backward, in small steps, in order for it to work best and, regardless of what you know, or think you know, you are being asked to accept, temporarily, the following premise:

Sometime in the 1st century, the gospels of Matthew, Mark, Luke and John were written in Ephesus, in Asia Minor (which today we call Turkey). The gospels were not four books. Instead, they were four columns on a single scroll, and they were penned in Greek by one man, not four. Let's say the author's name was John.

O.K., we can't be absolutely sure who wrote The Gospel. We can't even be sure his name was John and, if it was, whether he was Jesus' disciple or just some brilliant John Doe. It is common nowadays to credit a "John the Presbyter" or "John the Evangelist" with authorship.

We shouldn't be concerned, however, that the disciple John was the son of a fisherman, since common men have accomplished many of the world's great works. Think about that for a moment. And we shouldn't be concerned that the disciple would have been too old to write The Gospel, because we don't know exactly when it was written.

If you're looking for an authority, how about Irenaeus (c. 130-?), one of the fathers of the church who was purported to be a pupil of Polycarp, a disciple of John. Certainly, the late dates traditionally assigned to the gospels would make the disciple a very old man when he did the writing. On the other hand, if the traditional dates are wrong, it's another story. If it turns out that The Gospel was the earliest Christian writing, with everything else being written afterward, John the disciple easily could have been its author.

If Jesus was 35 or so when he was crucified – a claim for which there is absolutely no basis – John could hardly have been more than 15 years younger. But what if Jesus was closer to 50, as anybody called "rabbi" likely would have been? Jesus and John may not have been even close to the same age.

But what would make anyone think Jesus was 50 years old? Well, why would anyone think he was 35? The New Testament says Jesus was born at the time of a Roman census, but we know of no census even near Jesus' traditional birthdate. So we must look for another reference point. Consider this one:

Most people agree that when Jesus spoke about a temple that took 46 years to build and could be raised again in three days, it was a double entendre, meaning both Jerusalem's temple and Jesus' temple, or his body. Since none of the temples at Jerusalem took that long to build, could Jesus have meant that HIS temple, his body, was 46 years old?

Count back 46 years from the now generally accepted year of the crucifixion, A.D. 35, and you come up with 11 B.C. Remember the star over Bethlehem? In 12 and 11 B.C., Halley's Comet was making one of its infrequent (every 76 years) appearances and, according to reports throughout the Middle East, it was a spectacular one.

Anyway, if Jesus was born in the year of the comet, he would be 46 years old when he was killed. But who says John was the same age as Jesus? If John was around 25 then, he would be only 40 years old in the year 50 and 50 years old in the year 60. In the year 80, he still would only be 70. That would have been plenty of time to get the job done. Plus, at a time when boys became men at an early age, John could have been as young as 20. An exceptional man, and John certainly was one, might have written until the end of the 1st century.

The latter may be a bit of a stretch, but it's more ridiculous to dismiss the disciple out of hand.

The biggest reason we credit John with The Gospel, however, is because that's the name the earliest Christians associated with it. John was honored by name over many centuries, without any reference to anyone else – not Luke, Mark or Matthew, not anyone else.

By the way, if you like double entendres – and you should, because The Gospel is full of them – you might think about the passage that introduces the gospel bearing John's name, which is the first column on the scroll – the beginning of The Gospel ("In the beginning"). This is the restored passage:

"There was a man sent from God, whose name was John. The same came for a witness, to bear witness of the Light, that all men through him might believe."

Is that just about John the Baptist? Sure, we know, the Baptist lost his head.

O.K., enough of that. Now, you may be asking, "Why should we care so much about The Gospel?" Here's why:

First and foremost, the reason The Gospel ought to be all-important to ALL Christians is that it contains EVERYTHING that is known about Jesus. It is the ONLY source.

Some may ask, "Didn't Paul teach us about Jesus?" As their name indicates, Christians like to think of themselves as following Jesus the Christ. But through no fault of their own, vandalism of The Gospel has caused most Christians today to be more followers of Paul than of Jesus and regard the sacraments as more important than the Word. But regardless, they and all other Christians should be outraged over the sneak attack on Jesus 1,500 years ago and should want to resurrect his words.

Jesus and Paul complemented each other, if you will. Jesus taught us the truth through The Gospel. Paul taught little of what Jesus taught and he quoted nothing that is found in The Gospel, but he taught us how to build a church. So, there might not be a church without Paul, but there would be no Jesus without The Gospel. Think about that! Christianity without Christ! The rest of the New Testament is so much unneeded excelsior without Jesus.

Paul is not a huge problem in himself. The No. 1 problem is that 5th century vandals from Alexandria, Egypt, stole Paul's identity and used it in co-opting Jesus' Gospel. Their intent was to destroy or water down Jesus' words. You'll meet those culprits shortly.

To achieve their devious ends, the Egyptians fostered the myth that Paul's letters came BEFORE The Gospel of Jesus. They wanted us to believe that, before Paul, The Gospel of Jesus was merely an "oral tradition," a kind of rumor.

As you read further, it should become evident to you that while common people may not have known about John's Gospel, Paul – or whoever wrote Paul's letters and the Acts of the Apostles – DID know, and they DID have access to it.

These days, it is somewhat stylish – even among Christians – to wonder whether Jesus might not have been a fictional character, while the doubters are much more likely to accept that Paul was a historical figure. One television series about early Christianity quoted this outrageous suggestion: Christianity could have survived without Jesus, but it could not have survived without Paul. Of course, there's a grain of truth in it, if we're talking about churches surviving. But Christian churches without Christ?

Isn't it very amazing that Paul winds up being more believable than Jesus himself? Jesus was The Word, the universal truth, the Son of God! Paul was an apostle, and self-appointed, at that.

Just who was this Paul who stole Jesus' thunder? There were so few witnesses that he might as well have been invisible. A seemingly perfect person to ask about Paul would be Justin Martyr (c.100-c.165), who is regarded as the first great Christian apologist. He is said to have been born in Samaria, a Jew like Paul, converted in Ephesus around the year 138, and martyred in Rome. Justin Martyr followed in Paul's footsteps and, like Paul, wrote a lot that survives to this day.

So what did Justin Martyr have to say about Paul, who has been painted as the most important, most charismatic Christian who ever lived? He had this to say: NOTHING! He talked about The Gospel, but he had NOTHING to say about Paul! Why?

Likewise, none of the surviving writings by Papias contains any hint of Paul. Papias, bishop of Hierapolis in Asia Minor around the year 130, allegedly had been "hearer of John" and companion of Polycarp. Asia Minor supposedly was Paul's stomping ground and Paul visited Papias' cities of Hieropolis and Ephesus and such other nearby places as Laodicea, Philadelphia and Pisidian Antioch. But Papias was completely silent about Paul. Why?

Lucian of Samosata in Asia Minor (c.120-180) was a famous and prolific satirist of religions and philosophies, including Christianity, and authors such as Rabelais and Swift were to base works on his writing. Although Lucian covered much of the same ground that Paul trod only a few years before (in Asia Minor, Greece and Italy), he never mentioned Paul, either. Why?

Two of Christianity's staunchest enemies were Celsus, who wrote around the year 150, and Porphyry (c. 232-305). Neither mentioned Paul in any of his surviving writings, nor did any of those who knew Celsus or Porphyry. Even Justin, the apostate emperor who ruled around 360, practically ignored Paul in his anti-Christian writings. Those omissions indicate that Paul, if he existed at all, was not an important figure in the early years of Christianity.

Tertullian (c.155-223), considered by many to be the greatest theologian of the Western church before Augustine, failed to mention either Peter or Paul ever being in Rome. Josephus (c. 37-100), the famous Jewish historian and scholar, failed to mention Paul or Peter at all. And so on, and so on.

Far more significant is the fact that no fragment of any of Paul's works can be dated much before the 3rd century. And we are supposed to believe that his works pre-date John's Gospel. If Paul's letters actually were dispatched far and wide, as commonly believed, and treasured and copied extensively, as might be expected, why doesn't a single fragment of any letter survive from the early years? In contrast, early Gospel fragments have popped up all over Egypt. Again, why?

Of course, as they say, absence of evidence is not necessarily evidence of absence. But it's a good start.

So, why has the Christian church become Paul's church? What can we believe? We can believe Jesus. Paul's churches will take care of themselves; they always have.

There exists an amazing body of empirical evidence pointing to a conspiracy to steal Christianity from Jesus and give it to Paul and his successors. Yes, it's another plot! How fashionable!

First, however, we need to set the stage, which involves two other men possessing similar motives, but living about 300 years apart. The first is Marcion.

HALLEY'S COMET

(MOSTLY FOR FUN)

240 B.C.	First recorded by Chinese
11 B.C.	Jesus born?
66 A.D.	Seen as foretelling doom for Jerusalem
451 A.D.	Atilla the Hun defeated
1066 A.D.	Norman Conquest
1456 A.D.	Seen as favoring the feared Turks
1835 A.D.	Mark Twain born
1910 A.D.	Mark Twain dies
1986 A.D.	Most recent appearance

15

CONSIDER MARCION

*Since there is no evidence of Paul before Marcion,
could Paul have been Marcion's pen name?*

E arly in the 2nd century, there was a man named Marcion who lived at Sinop on the Black Sea coast of Asia Minor (Turkey). He is known chiefly for compiling the earliest known New Testament canon. Canon is what we call a list of accepted holy scriptures.

Marcion's canon consisted only of "The Gospel of the Lord," actually a heavily altered gospel of Luke with references to Judaism removed, plus parts of 10 epistles or letters attributed to Paul. The letters were Galatians, with which Marcion identified strongly; Corinthians I and II; Romans I and II; Thessalonians; Ephesians, which he called Laodicians; Colossians; Phillipians, and Philemon.

Tertullian (c. 155-225), the Christian apologist and writer, would charge that "Marcion expressly and openly used the knife, not the pen, since he made such an excision of the scriptures as suited his own subject matter."

Marcion maintained that the Christian scriptures rendered Hebrew law (that is, the Ten Commandments) irrelevant. Marcion's canon, which omitted the Jewish scriptures and included only Christian writings, marks the split between Christianity and Judaism. His canon, moreover, also didn't list Matthew, Mark, John, Acts, Revelation and the other letters.

It is interesting to speculate about the various omissions, but it is the inclusion of the 10 Paulian epistles that is especially interesting. That's because it is from Marcion that we hear about Paul the very first time (Please remember this).

Church historians say Marcion was a wealthy shipowner and son of the bishop of Sinop. We are told he had many enemies, and it's no wonder; he was the kind of heretic who gives heretics a bad name. Contending that the God of the Jews was evil and vindictive, Marcion just couldn't accept that such an ogre could be the father of Jesus.

A lot of people felt that way, as they do today, but Marcion's solution was the problem. While conceding that the Hebrew God did indeed create everything, Marcion further postulated that there had to be another, more benevolent God who was the father of Jesus. But he didn't do a good job of explaining how that could be.

Although we're not sure exactly when either Paul or Marcion lived, both supposedly were active in Asia Minor during the second half of the 1st century. Even if Marcion didn't meet Paul, he could be expected to have known all about Paul, especially since the two men shared the same milieu.

As a shipowner, Marcion was involved in trade, and logically called at all of the cities Paul is said to have visited along the Aegean and Mediterranean coasts of Asia Minor, such as Troas, Assos, Ephesus, Cnidus, Myra, Patara, Attalia and Tarsus. Palestine was just beyond. We know, too, that Marcion went to Rome. Like Paul, he undoubtedly could tell a sea story or two.

As son of the bishop of Sinop and, according to church historians, himself a sort-of bishop at large, Marcion probably also visited, or was familiar with, some of the Christian communities of the interior. Regions mentioned by Paul – Pontus, Galatia, Bithynia, Pamphylia and Cappadocia – were all reasonably within Marcion's range, and some of their Christian inhabitants no doubt were actually his father's personal responsibilities.

And being involved in trade, Marcion quite logically traveled the major caravan routes that brought goods to the important port of Sinop to be transshipped on his vessels. Paul's Tarsus and John's Ephesus were at the other ends of major caravan routes leading northward, through Angora (the modern Ankara), to Sinop. Tarsus was on the Mediterranean and Ephesus on the Aegean.

It might be noted here that Angora was the capital of Galatia, in northern Asia Minor, yet Galatia ended up on Paul's itineraries and correspondence list, which otherwise consisted only of towns in southern Asia Minor and along the southern and western coasts. Scholars always have been puzzled by that. Marcion, on the other hand, must have been familiar with Galatia and Angora. His charter, in fact, was Paul's Epistle to the Galatians, which showed contempt for Jewish law.

The capper is this: The Gospel was written in the great Asia Minor city of Ephesus not long before Marcion came along. Marcion is said to have been born as early as the year 70 and to have lived until around the year 150. Could he have met John, or at least have had access to the original Gospel? With his and/or his father's credentials, Marcion logically could have seen and handled the scroll. Could he have managed to copy one column (that of Luke) and abridge it for his own use?

It may be interesting to note that there are present-day admirers of Marcion who believe he actually wrote the "Gospel of the Lord" that he included in his canon – perhaps even with Paul's assistance – and that Luke copied his gospel from Marcion's, rather than vice versa.

Marcion's people consider it significant that most parallel passages in Luke are a bit longer than those in Marcion's gospel, suggesting to them that Luke embroidered on what Marcion had said. Even if we didn't know better, the much greater likelihood would be that Marcion developed writer's cramp and paraphrased Luke, using fewer words. To give the devil his due, Marcion must be praised for limiting himself to crimes of omission, avoiding crimes of commission.

The writer of Luke couldn't have copied from Marcion, for two reasons. First, because the secret patterns contained in the gospel of Luke forever tie Luke to Matthew, Mark and John. Second, because almost every word in Marcion's gospel is also in Luke, Marcion's gospel couldn't have been composed independently of the four-fold Gospel. Anyway, Luke didn't write Luke, John wrote Luke – along with Matthew, Mark and John.

We owe Marcion a small debt for the first New Testament canon, despite his anti-Semitic leanings, but we also owe him for some clues he inadvertently gave us about the original Gospel. If he DID paraphrase the Luke column he found in John's original manuscript (which, again, included John, Luke, Mark and Matthew, side by side), why didn't he include the first two chapters of Luke as we know it? There are other, smaller, but important "omissions," as well. An educated guess is that he didn't copy them from John's scroll because he didn't see them. And the reason he didn't see them is because THEY WEREN'T THERE!

The Jesus in Marcion's version of the gospel of Luke was never a babe or a youth, as he was in the book of Luke that has come down to us. In the first sentence of Marcion's gospel, Jesus is already an adult: "Now, in the fifteenth year of Tiberius Caesar, Pontius Pilate being governor of Judaea, Jesus, the Son of God, came down from heaven and appeared at Capernaum, a town in Galilee." Who wrote the first two chapters of Luke, when were they written, and why?

History tells us, at any rate, that Marcion founded a church that lasted 500 years, and he is still regarded by many to have been the most dangerous "heretic" Christianity ever faced. Like Paul, he was contemptuous of the Jews and their religion, felt that Christians needn't follow Jewish law (i.e. the Ten Commandments), had disdain for women, and so forth. Marcion's agenda was Paul's agenda, and Paul's was Marcion's.

Since there is no evidence of Paul prior to Marcion, could Paul have started out as merely the pen name of Marcion?

'PAUL'S GOSPEL'

(THE WORDS OF GOD?)

- "God gave (the Jews) a spirit of stupor, eyes that should not see and ears that should not hear, down to this very day" (Romans)
- "It is good for a man not to touch a woman" (I Corinthians)
- "Let your women keep silence in the churches… And if they will learn any thing, let them ask their husbands at home" (I Corinthians)
- "Wives, be subject to your husbands, as is fitting in the Lord" (Colossians)
- "Let every soul be subject unto the higher powers (any earthly authority)" (Romans)
- "If any one is preaching to you a gospel contrary to that which you received, let him be accursed" (Galatians)
- "I wish those who unsettle you would mutilate themselves!" (Galatians)
- "…Let her wear a veil. (A man) is the image and the glory of God; but woman is the glory of man" (I Corinthians)
- "If any one will not work, let him not eat" (II Thessalonians)

16

ALEXANDRIA THE MAGNIFIC

It is too bad that ancient Alexandria has been largely forgotten by the Western world. It can be said that the Western mind was born there.

Founded by Alexander the Great in 332 B.C., that magnificent Egyptian city was ruled by the Ptolemys, a line of Graeco-Egyptian kings, until the Romans took over in 31 B.C. In the early centuries of the Christian era, Alexandria was the cultural capital of the world.

The city's most important asset was the Mouseion (Museum) of Ptolemy I Soter. The Mouseion, from which all of the world's museums take their name, wasn't, however, merely a place where objects were preserved and displayed; it was a university famous for its contributions to science, philosophy, mathematics, literature and art. It boasted by far the world's largest library – as many as 700,000 volumes – and the Didascaleion, the famous Alexandrian catechetical school, oldest in the world.

Alexandria was home to the likes of Archimedes, Erasistratos, Eratosthenes, Euclid, Herophilus, Theocritus and Zenodotus.

It is estimated that by the 1st century A.D. the city had about half a million free inhabitants, among them Egyptians, Greeks, Romans, Ethiopians, Nubians, Persians, Babylonians, Indians and, according to the historian Gibbon, perhaps 40,000 Jews – almost as many Jews as Greeks.

Dazzling marble temples, palaces and monuments were everywhere. The great lighthouse of Alexandria, one of the Seven Wonders of the World, would stand until the end of the 8th century. The purported tomb of Alexander was in the city, and crowds cheered as Cleopatra and Julius Caesar strolled hand-in-hand through the streets.

So what does Alexandria have to do with Christianity? Western church history short-changes Alexandria like it short-changes Asia Minor (today's Turkey). It is accurate to say that Christianity was born in Asia Minor, because that's where a man probably named John wrote The Gospel, and Paul or someone else wrote the earliest epistles attributed to Paul. But church doctrine, as we know it, originated neither in the Holy Land, nor Asia Minor, nor Rome, but in Egypt.

Church doctrine was shaped in Alexandria, at the Didascaleion, by famous men like Clement, Origen, Athanasius, Athenagoras, Didymus and Arius.

Christianity had come fairly early to Egypt. The Coptic Church even claims that St. Mark came to Egypt just a dozen years after the crucifixion. Then, with the founding of the catechetical school around the year 190 the city became the leading center of Christian thought.

Alexandria's influence allowed its patriarchs eventually to overcame every single opponent to its orthodoxy. Athanasius destroyed Arius, father of the so-called Arian heresy; Cyril destroyed Nestorius, father of the so-called Nestorian heresy; Theophilus destroyed Chrysostom, whose heresy, incidentally, was of the worst possible kind, in the eyes of the Alexandrians. That's because Chrysostom refused the rich accouterments of high office, preached against injustice and inequality and funneled church revenues into charities. He loved the people, and the people loved him.

While all of that speaks volumes about the Alexandrian school, the same folks also gave us the New Testament in its final form, warts and all.

The fact that the New Testament originated in Alexandria comes as a shock to most Christians. It shouldn't, however, be difficult to imagine if you know that the Old Testament with which most of us are familiar was born in the city 500 years earlier. Of course, few know that, either.

"Our" Old Testament is based on the Septuagint, the famous translation of the Hebrew scriptures into Greek that was started in Alexandria in the 3rd century B.C. That translation, probably completed sometime in the 1st century B.C., was needed because, by that time, few Jews of the Diaspora could any longer speak or read Hebrew. Their language was Greek.

All subsequent translations depended on the work of those Alexandrian rabbis (legend says there were 72), which actually made the Greek Septuagint the original of most ancient versions of the Old Testament. Although Jews later abandoned the Septuagint, without it the world would have lost a lot of the Hebrew Bible, and there would be many more errors in what remained.

So, the city that gave us both the Old and New Testaments came to wield enough authority to win out not only over every major heresy, but over the rival churches of Antioch, imperial Constantinople and Rome, plus a bunch of interfering emperors who thought they were annointed by God.

Then, drunk with power, the Alexandrians committed one of the worst crimes in history. They eviscerated The Gospel of Jesus the Christ, and that's going to be our main concern here.

In case you wondered, there's a reason the world has forgotten both Alexandria's glories and its predations. Although the city emerged as the undisputed, practically undefeated ruler of the Christian world, its reign of omnipotence was prematurely and abruptly cut short when Islam overran Alexandria, Antioch, Jerusalem and Constantinople.

The Muslim conquest rewrote history. Because Rome was the only major Christian center to escape Muslim invaders, it inherited by default everything the brilliant Egyptian church had created. Rome fell heir both to the New Testament in its final form and to a ready-made doctrine that would change little over the next 1,500 years.

17

PETER, PAUL IN ROME?

They could be described as a riddle wrapped in a mystery inside an enigma

Origen, who has been called the father of theology, was born in Alexandria and eventually became bishop and head of the catechetical school there. Around 220, he compiled a list, or canon, of "generally recognized" Christian writings that contained the "four gospels," 13 epistles of Paul, 1 Peter, 1 John, Revelation, and The Acts of the Apostles.

In 367, Athanasius, another bishop of Alexandria and another product of its catechetical school, declared the New Testament canon fixed, and it remains unchanged to this day. Athanasius' canon also included II and III John, II Peter, Jude, James, and the Epistle to the Hebrews.

It is significant that it was in the great Greco-Egyptian city of Alexandria that the scriptures took on their final form, not in Rome, whose claim to importance is based solely on the tradition that Peter and Paul were there.

Some scholars doubt, however, that either Peter or Paul ever reached Rome, and believe Christians didn't arrive in any great numbers until much later. They point out that in Rome's catacombs no tombs dating from before the year 200 appear to be Christian. Tertullian (c. 155-225), who is considered the greatest theologian in the Western (Roman) church before Augustine, doesn't mention either Peter or Paul being in Rome.

The only reason to believe Christians might have been present in Rome in any numbers before the 3rd century is a single reference attributed to the historian Publius Cornelius Tacitus (c. 56-117), describing the Emperor Nero's actions following the burning of the city in the year 64. Thanks to Hollywood, scenes based on that lone source – of Christians being fed to animals, crucified and used as human torches – are seared into our minds. Especially vivid are pictures of Peter and Paul being martyred in Rome, even though Tacitus mentions neither.

A single, brief mention of Christians by the Jewish historian Josephus (c. 37-100) is generally conceded by scholars to be a Christian interpolation. Furthermore, there is no mention of Christians anywhere for 50 more years, not until Pliny the Younger writes about them as being a problem in Bithynia, in Asia Minor. By that time, any mention of Jesus or Christians is more likely to be Christian propaganda than an unbiased account.

So why was Tacitus the only one to notice Christians in Rome and, having noticed, why did he have so little to say about them – and nothing at all about Peter or Paul?

To borrow what Winston Churchill once said about Russia, Peter and Paul are "a riddle wrapped in a mystery inside an enigma."

While it is not absolutely crucial to this treatise to prove that Christian activity in Rome was minimal in the early years, the absence of evidence is a big puzzle, especially with such supposedly charismatic figures as Peter and Paul leading the way. Again, the absence of evidence is not necessarily evidence of absence, but it raises a red flag. So, the following is offered as one possible explanation for the paragraph that inspired so many Hollywood spectaculars. You are not expected to accept the theory without question, but it may give you something to think about.

There was another Tacitus – Marcus Claudius Tacitus (c. 200-276) – who was 75 years old when he became emperor of Rome in 275, and he died just six months later. Because of his brief reign, his name doesn't even appear in some lists of Roman rulers, although he bore an already famous name. The emperor was a proud descendant of Publius Cornelius Tacitus, the renowned historian and intimate friend of Pliny the Younger who supposedly wrote the bit about the Christians in the arena.

His short reign notwithstanding, history tells us that Marcus Claudius still managed to find time to put the works of ancestor Publius Cornelius in all of the public libraries and order them to be transcribed 10 times a year at public expense.

Might we suspect that some changes were made in the manuscripts as they were being copied? It is, indeed, reasonable to expect that. We know that amost every time there was opportunity and power (such as emperors and bishops had), books were routinely revised before being copied.

It was especially easy to revise history in those days before printing, because every book started out as a single manuscript as, for instance, did The Gospel. Contemporaries tell us that ancient libraries were filled with scrolls and books that, because of forgeries and other vandalism, had been turned into patchwork quilts. Some of the Dead Sea Scrolls, for example, are much-patched.

It would be interesting to see what the Emperor Marcus Claudius Tacitus would have done next, but he soon retired to an impossibly small and remote place called Tyana in Cappadocia, Asia Minor, where he died, reportedly of exhaustion. We can't be certain, but it is logical that the emperor went to small and remote Tyana to die because it was his childhood home, and an educated guess would be that his ancestor, Publius Cornelius Tacitus, also came from Tyana. Alas, the historian didn't tell us about himself.

Worth noting is that little Tyana's favorite son was neither the historian nor the emperor. It was the celebrated neo-Pythagorean philosopher known as Apollonius of Tyana, considered by some to be the greatest religious figure of his time, greater even than Jesus. Tradition says Apollonius was born in A.D. 1. According to some more extravagant accounts, he was the son of a mortal woman and an Egyptian god, which resonates, of course, with the Christian tradition.

Disregarding any miracles that may, or may not, have surrounded his birth, Apollonius was a historical figure. He wandered throughout the Roman Empire and beyond, teaching, supposedly performing miracles, and living until about the year 97. Many temples were dedicated to him, and some of his admirers claim Jesus was modeled after the philosopher. Some Christians, of course, counter that Apollonius copied Jesus. In either case, their messages weren't much alike, and it's the message – not the miracles – that counts, isn't it? Well, isn't it?

Does this leave you wanting to know more about Apollonius of Tyana? Well, O.K., but you should know that he had a terrific press agent. Most of what we know about him was written by Philostratus (170-245) about two centuries after Apollonius lived. Philostratus, a rhetorician, was commissioned by the Roman Empress Julia Domna, second wife of Septimius Severus, to write Apollonius' biography.

By the 2nd century, the appeal of the old gods had been waning for some time, and Romans were shopping for new religions such as that of Apollonius. Julia Domna herself was daughter of the high priest of the Syrian god Elagabalus. Her son, the cruel Caracalla, preferred the pseudo-Egyptian god Serapis, even pretending to be either Serapis' brother or son. Serapis – whose image was modeled after a colossus of a Greek god in Marcion's hometown of Sinop – was an ersatz diety manufactured by the Romans expressly for the Egyptians.

A nephew of Julia Domna, who bore the same name as the Syrian god Elagabalus, became the Roman Emperor Elagabalus in 218. The mortal Elagabalus, who had been reared in Syria as a hereditary priest, is said to have liked to dress in women's clothing, paint his face, pose as a prostitute, and walk on carpets of roses and lilies. Alexander Severus, another of Julia Domna's nephews, who succeeded Elagabalus as emperor, followed his aunt's lead. He, too, venerated Apollonius of Tyana.

Could an empress with Julia Domna's background, an admirer of Apollonius, be hostile toward Christians, who refused to worship pagan gods? Of course she could.

And might not the Emperor Tacitus, out of loyalty to his hometown's illustrious son, Apollonius, be tempted to implicate Jesus' followers in the burning of Rome? Why not? In the Christian vignette ascribed to historian Publius Cornelius Tacitus, Christians are called "a race of men detested for their evil practices," and their religion "a dangerous superstition." They were convicted, according to the passage, "not indeed on clear evidence of having set the city on fire, but rather on account of their sullen hatred of the whole human race."

Does that sound like Christians? Does that sound objective? It is the kind of bias that, if he had one, any serious historian would try to conceal, and Tacitus is considered the greatest Roman historian. So, did the historian actually write that passage about Christians, or is it perhaps the work of his imperial namesake? An emperor would have no commitment at all to objectivity. Plus, early Christians came largely from the lowest classes which, in itself, would cloud the judgment of any emperor or empress.

18

THEOPHILUS AND CYRIL

"If 50 million people say a foolish thing, it is still a foolish thing"

— Anatole France

While there is no evidence that Paul was ever in Rome, multiple sources agree that Marcion of Sinop was there. Just as Marcion was intimately familiar with Paul's Asia Minor and its Aegean and Mediterranean coasts, he also knew all about Rome, having lived there.

You will remember that it was from Marcion that we heard about Paul for the first time, and that it was Marcion who included parts of 10 Pauline epistles in the first known New Testament canon. Again, did Marcion know Paul, as some have suggested? Or could Marcion have written those 10 Pauline letters himself?

While we're questioning Paul's letters, we might point out that the source of the novel-like Acts of the Apostles is just as hazy. We DO know that Acts was of mysterious origin, a very late-bloomer, and lightly regarded in the early years. One reason we know that is because of what John Chrysostom, bishop of Constantinople, said around the year 400, almost two centuries AFTER Origen included the book in his canon. "To many persons," Chrysostom said, "this book (Acts) is so little known, both it and its author, that they are not even aware that there is such a book in existence."

Wow! Was he really talking about the same book of Acts whose authorship would be credited to Luke, and which has been tied so securely to The Gospel through the book of Luke that it is often referred to as "Part II of the book of Luke-Acts"? Was he talking about the same book of Acts that has become the charter, the cornerstone of many Christian churches? Instead of The Gospel?

Who was this John Chrysostom, anyway? John, a deacon and priest at Antioch who lived between 347 and 407, has been described as THE most prominent doctor of the Greek church and the greatest Christian preacher who ever lived. Strangely then, after being ordained bishop of Constantinople by the Patriarch Theophilus of Alexandria, he was condemned and exiled at Theophilus' instigation at the Synod of the Oak in the year 403. What did John do to deserve that? Had he become a threat to the Alexandrian school?

John Chrysostom's puzzlement over the Book of Acts leads one to suspect that Acts was concocted by the Alexandrian school expressly to tie together the disparate scriptural elements that would become our New Testament.

A very good reason to doubt the early importance, or even the authenticity, of Acts is that fact that it was not mentioned anywhere by Sozomen, the 5th century historian, in the nine-volume history of the church that he wrote and dedicated to the Emperor Theodosius II.

An important figure at the Synod of the Oak, where the greatly popular John Chrysostom was destroyed, was Theophilus' nephew, Cyril, who would succeed his uncle as bishop of Alexandria after a riot involving Cyril's followers and those of his rival.

Mark well the name of Cyril, because he's the main conspirator in the assault on The Gospel, taking up where Marcion left off. Evidence points to Cyril as having stolen the original Gospel manuscript and having written the phony dedications to his uncle Theophilus ("most excellent Theophilus") at the beginning of both the gospel of Luke and the book of Acts. That made it seem that a man named Luke, supposedly a friend of Paul, had written both Luke and Acts expressly for Theophilus and handed them directly to him.

Unfortunately, the canard that a man named Luke authored "Luke-Acts" has been repeated for so many centuries that it is now usually accepted without question. But it needs to be questioned. To paraphrase Anatole France, even if 50 million people say that something untrue is true, it's still untrue.

During most of man's history everyone also believed the earth was flat – until it was proved to be otherwise. And a few Christians still believe Archbishop James Ussher's reckoning that the world was created on Oct. 26, 4004 B.C. at 10 in the morning, an absurdity that once was even printed in the margins of Bibles (speaking of tares).

The fact, therefore, that so many generations couldn't figure out that the Theophilus mentioned in Luke and Acts was the 5th century bishop shouldn't be surprising. It is a tribute to the vandals' chutzpah. Ordinary people had a poor sense of how much time had elapsed between the age of the apostles and their own, had never seen the scriptures and never would see them. So Cyril brazenly planted the forgeries that intimated that his mentor, Theophilus, had received the gospel of Luke separately and possibly directly from its alleged putative author.

Today, we have a far better idea of time, although the leading opinion, based on nothing, is still that Theophilus probably was some first-century official whom Luke was trying to impress. One particularly fatuous notion is that Theophilus was merely a literary device, similar to the ones authors used a hundred years ago – like "Dear kind and gentle reader."

But again, the Theophilus whom Cyril wrote into Luke and Acts was 5th century bishop of Alexandria. He, Cyril and other Egyptians perverted The Gospel for their own purposes, blinding Christians for 1,500 years, up to this very day. Their dirty work, which may seem relatively harmless at first glance, has justified unspeakable offenses in Jesus' name over the centuries – by no means limited to the Holocaust, colonialism, slavery, the Inquisition, the Crusades, and the burning of "witches" and books. Unchanged, it will continue to be used by evil people looking for an excuse to be evil and blame Jesus.

Had Theophilus and Cyril done anything in their earlier years to presage the violence they did to the Bible? Yes, plenty. Theophilus had destroyed the temples of Dionysius, Mithra, and Serapis throughout North Africa, and even the Serapeum of Alexandria, which was repository of the largest collection of books surviving from the classical age. Theophilus also led the troops who destroyed the Origenist Christian monks' desert monasteries and, as we have noted, caused the condemnation and exile of the good John Chrysostom.

Cyril had a similar record and his victims, like those of Theophilus, were diverse. In the year 414, he presided over history's first recorded pogrom against the Jews, ending with their exile from Alexandria. He closed the Novatian churches; instigated the murder of Hypatia, the famous Neoplatonist philosopher; dissolved the Sanhedrin, and closed the Jewish academies in Galilee.

St. Cyril, patriarch of Alexandria, thief and murderer, seems to be taunting us by wearing vestment and miter covered with crosses. The cross is the key to restoring The Gospel, which he stole and vandalized. This ghastly portrait is part of an 11th century fresco.

Cyril succeeded in deposing Nestorius at the Council of Ephesus (431), which had been called by the emperor to settle the dispute between the two bishops. Nestorius' biggest mistake was opposing Cyril's insistence that Mary, the mother of Jesus, be recognized as Mother of God. A deified Mary would please Cyril's Egyptian constituents, whose ancestors worshipped a father-mother-son trinity of Osiris, Isis and Horus.

History tells us that Cyril saw his chance to get the drop on the Nestorians by arriving early at Ephesus. A bunch of thugs who accompanied him fomented a riot and, in the confusion, Cyril did as he had done in the Novatian churches and elsewhere. He seized the sacred objects of the Temple of the Theotokos or the Temple of John. Our belief is that the most sacred treasure in the temple was the original Gospel scroll penned by John (along with I John) and its theft CHANGED CHRISTIANITY FOREVER.

It is frustrating when historical accounts are lost, one example being the afore-mentioned work of 5th-century historian Sozomen. Born of Greek Christian parents in what is now the Gaza Strip, Sozomen wrote a nine-volume history of the church covering the years 312 to 439, and dedicated it to the Emperor Theodosius II.

Unfortunately, the years 425 through 439 are missing. They were probably removed by Maximian, patriarch of Constantinople, after both Theodosius and Sozomen died in the same year (450).

Sozomen's history would have helped answer many questions: About how Cyril manipulated the Council of Ephesus, about the riot in the temple, the fate of John's manuscript, the Mary controversy, Cyril's fight with Nestorius, and Maximian's victory over Cyril.

19

WHO'S WHO, WHAT'S WHAT?

This could be slightly distracting here, but to make sure we're still on the same page, so to speak, the following definitions of terms are offered:

Cyril, or the culprit?

It is tempting to blame Cyril completely for vandalizing The Gospel since, having stolen the original scroll, he richly deserves the honor. But it's always a mistake to simplify history by personifying it, as we do when we say "Hitler" seized the Sudentenland or "Hitler" set up the death camps. Others played roles.

We sometimes refer to the bad guys as members of the Alexandrian school, the Egyptians, or the Alexandrian gang. Cyril, Theophilus and associates sounds too much like a law firm, but forgers, counterfeiters, tare sowers, culprits, thieves, murderers or thugs all seem justifiable. Since the church later saw fit to canonize the principal perpetrators, we also like calling them holy vandals, or just vandals for short. After 1,500 years, we can't libel them. Who said life is fair?

a gospel, or The Gospel?

You already may have noticed an inconsistent treatment of the word gospel. When we're talking about John's original four-fold manuscript – four parallel columns on a single scroll – we refer to it as The Gospel, with upper-case "T" and "G".

When we're talking about a "separated gospel" – that is, one of the four columns slit from the scroll and given the names Matthew, Mark, Luke and John – we use a lower-case G, thus: "gospel" or the "gospel of Mark" or the "book of Luke."

John the disciple or John Doe?

As we agreed earlier, when we talk about the author of The Gospel, we say John, and you can decide for yourself whether it's John the disciple, John the Presbyter, John the Evangelist or some incredibly brilliant John Doe. Sometimes we just refer to him as the author.

Books or scrolls?

And since there were both books and scrolls by the 5th century, sometimes we just say books, when we mean books AND scrolls.

Speaking of books and scrolls, if it were possible to show in the pages of this book all of the vandalism that has been done to the Bible, it would be a very thick book indeed. Anyway, it isn't possible. Some of the switches in text are multiple switches, even between chapters and "gospels." In a few cases, John created the outlines of trees and other objects out of words, and they are too large to be shown on book pages.

For any who might want to go beyond this book, it will be possible. John's entire Gospel has been re-created in scroll form and in English! It may come as a shock, but the scroll actually was completely restored 25 years ago, but not published, because it would have been technically too difficult and too expensive at that time.

Such printing, however, recently has become both technologically and economically feasible, and the restored scroll is now being prepared for printing, as well as for computer display. The scroll and explanatory text will be available within months.

20

VOTING ON GOD

"Power tends to corrupt, and absolute power corrupts absolutely. Great men are almost always bad men."

–Lord Acton

Modern Christians need to understand that much of Christian doctrine is not based on the Bible – not even loosely. From the very beginning, Christians didn't agree on what the scriptures meant, and the various factions were as rabid as today's sports fans.

Common people quarreled in the streets of Constantinople and Alexandria about whether Jesus was a man or God or something in between. Some argued that the crucifixion, death and resurrection were real; some said symbolic. The churches were equally tendentious and, to settle disputes, emperors called councils of church bishops. And the emperors had their favorites.

Huge questions like the ones we cited were decided by vote, like modern Americans decide on the No. 1 football team, or school levies or who gets a license to sell liquor. But the stakes in those days were higher. Losers sometimes were anathematized, exiled or even slain, so 15 centuries later, right or wrong, we're stuck with all of those council votes. Even today, there are theologians who think the good guys ALWAYS LOST.

Whether the right side always lost, or just sometimes lost, the point is this: The Gospel may have come to us from on high, because it is pure truth, but the interpretation of it – church doctrine – did not. Fifteen hundred years ago men made various interpretations of the scriptures, voted on them, then told us we had no right to question the outcome.

The Ecumenical Council of Ephesus in 431 is a good example of the ungodly nature of the councils in which Christian doctrine was decided.

The influence of the Alexandrian church had grown steadily; the Nicene Creed, for example, was authored by the Patriarch Athanasius. By 431, Theophilus and Cyril of Alexandria had amassed so much power that they were ready to take over Christianity, separate it from its Hebrew roots, and steer it away from Jesus. The telling blow, it turned out, would be facilitated by a woman named Pulcheria, the elder sister of the emperor in Constantinople.

Cyril had a brilliant but simple plan. He would persuade the Emperor Theodosius II to call an ecumenical council at Ephesus, the acknowledged capital of Christianity. He would use the meeting to destroy his rivals at Antioch and Constantinople in one swift blow, then he would steal John's original Gospel scroll.

History tells us that Cyril first approached Pulcheria through a eunuch in the harem, after which she prevailed on Theodosius to call the Council of 431. That council would prove to be the pivotal event in the history of the Christian church.

Theodosius was an indolent ruler. Pulcheria had acted as regent until Theodosius came of age, but then stayed on as co-ruler. While Arcadius, the father of Theodosius and Pulcheria, had favored the Antioch church over the one at Alexandria, Pulcheria hated the Antiochean church, including Cyril's enemy Nestorius, who had come from Antioch to become patriarch of Constantinople, the capital of the empire.

Like Cyril, Pulcheria was a staunch advocate of Mary, having built three churches in Constantinople and having dedicated them to her. Her devotion to Mary no doubt endeared her to Cyril.

The big loser in the great war of the churches was Nestorius who, at that point in history, represented both the church of the imperial city of Constantinople and that of his native Antioch. Those were two of the three great cities of the time, the other being Alexandria. Cyril, whom Theodosius put in charge of the meeting at Ephesus, used his position of power to get Nestorius condemned and anathematized before Nestorius' Antioch supporters even arrived. Nestorius would be exiled to Cyril's Egypt, then forced to flee from place to place until his death in 440.

The Antioch church had always emphasized Jesus' human side, thus conflicting with the Alexandrian view that Jesus was God, period. Nestorius' chief mistake, therefore, was opposing Cyril's insistence that Mary, the mother of Jesus, be recognized as Mother of God. A deified Mary would please Cyril's Egyptian constituents, whose ancestors had worshipped the father-mother-son trinity of Osiris, Isis and Horus. So Cyril spread word that the reason Nestorius didn't believe Mary was mother of God was that he didn't believe Jesus was God. Nestorius found himself in a lose-lose situation. The entire future of Christianity turned on semantics.

Then Cyril stole the scroll. He knew that if he possessed the only copy of the complete, four-fold Gospel, he could make Christianity anything he wanted to make it.

One person who was told about *The Crisscross Double-Cross* in its beginning stages said something like this: "You are painting the fathers of the church as mean-spirited. Sure, some of them may have hated the Jews, and even hated the Hebrew God, in a way, but how can you say they had contempt for Jesus and his teachings? They all were professed Christians!"

Again, Jesus was no Christian; he was a Jew. But yes, the early church fathers were professed Christians, and more. They professed to be direct, even recent heirs of the apostles themselves or their immediate successors. Forget that the apostles had died 300 years before.

People weren't yet slaves to calendars in the 4th and 5th centuries. Calendars were a guide to when the Nile would flood and when it was time to till, sow and harvest. The year 1, the supposed year of Jesus' birth, wasn't calculated until hundreds of years later, so people in the 5th century didn't know whether the current year was 431 or 131. They had no real sense of elapsed time. Not until the Council of Nicaea in 325 was even the landmark date for Easter decided upon.

Nearly 400 years had passed. The holy vandals weren't any closer in time to Jesus and his disciples than we are to Shakespeare and King James of England, who lived 400 years before our time. People like Theophilus and Cyril may have been canonized in later years, but they weren't holy by virtue of being closely associated with Jesus or his apostles, or with the apostles' disciples, or with anyone even remotely related to them. In other words, they weren't special, except in their own minds.

Christianity, to the holy vandals, was a power game that already had been going on for centuries and, by the 5th century, Jesus had become merely a pawn in their game.

Those were ordinary men, and they weren't interested in loving their neighbor or much of anything Jesus taught – least of all, the Ten Commandments. We know for certain how they felt about Jesus' teachings because of what they did to the Bible to obscure them.

The vandals' attitude toward Jesus was love-hate at best, and it was a user relationship at worst. The vandals used Jesus as an excuse to build a church whose main purpose wasn't Jesus' teachings, but the aggrandizement and enrichment of its clergy. They used Jesus' name, but mostly in the performance of rituals. Magic and miracles are the refuge of those who either don't understand Jesus' teachings, or don't want to.

So many pagan practices were adopted that Christianity became almost indistinguishable from other religions. Many pagan practices remain today, including fasting, celibacy, image and relic worship, consecrated water, miracles, festivals, including the celebration of the winter solstice (Christmas), appeasing the dead with wine and feasts, and turning martyrs into idols. Priests still wear rich robes, miters and tiaras and carry candles and gold and silver objects in procession. An Egyptian-style trinity is worshiped in some circles, with the image of Isis holding the infant Horus morphing into Madonna and Child.

More on the question of mean-spiritedness. Although they committed many evil acts, there's no evidence that Cyril and his friends were anti-Jesus. They would have been outraged by such a suggestion, but it's easy to guess what they were thinking. They told themselves that they were helping Jesus overcome an evil, pagan world by building an invincible church, against which the gates of hell could not prevail.

Like most of the rest of us, however, the Alexandrian evildoers were only nominal Christians, loving Jesus' miracles perhaps too much, and never truly loving the teachings that the miracles were meant to illustrate. That is, they were too self-centered to love their neighbors and too selfish to do many good deeds; they were generally lacking in truth and grace. The difference between them and us is that they possessed power unequaled in the history of Christianity.

Cyril's people are easy to understand. As they grew older and piled success atop success, they became more and more impressed with themselves. Predictably, they ended up concluding that they must have been chosen by God and, in their task of church-building, they would stop at nothing. They had a commission from God.

It's as Lord Acton would observe: Power tends to corrupt, and absolute power corrupts absolutely.

21

ENTER ROME AND JEROME

Today, the Roman Catholic Church claims primacy which, according to the dictionary, means "first and foremost."

Despite its pretensions, however, the church in Rome didn't become first and foremost until rather late, not until the 5th century, at the Council of Ephesus in 431, which was presided over by Cyril of Alexandria.

The Egyptian patriarchs had become weary of battling the sees of Antioch and Constantinople and particularly tired of the uncertain influence of the Byzantine emperors, who got involved not only in the hiring and firing of bishops, but in the shaping of Christian doctrine.

So, Cyril made a brilliant move – and end run – by forging an alliance with Rome. Although Rome had never been the major force in the Christian movement, the bishop of Rome, the pope, had the advantage of not being under the nose of the emperor or the emperor's personal bishop.

The picture of the future became clear when the Council of 431 banished Nestorius, Cyril's chief nemesis. After the council smote Nestorius, an unlikely voice delivered the summation. The Roman legate Philip announced that the action had been taken "canonically and in accordance with ecclesiastical learning" and, "conformably with the instructions of the most holy pope, Celestine." Then Philip made this historic pronouncement:

"No one doubts, nay it is a thing known now for centuries, that the holy and most blessed Peter, the prince and head of the apostles, the pillar of the faith and the foundation on which the Catholic Church is built, received from Our Lord, Jesus Christ, the saviour and redeemer of the human race, the keys of the kingdom, and that to him there was given the power of binding and of loosing from sin; who, down to this day, and for evermore, lives and exercises judgment in his successors."

In reality, Peter wasn't recognized as the first bishop of Rome until the late 2nd or early 3rd century. All bishops and priests then claimed to be Peter's successors, and the Roman clergy claimed to be his DIRECT successors. The tradition that Peter had been in Rome eventually became so strong that not even an emperor dared question it. By invoking the old tradition, Cyril not only had got the emperor out of his hair, but he insured that the Alexandrian school, through Rome, its proxy, would determine the shape of Christianity for all time.

There was acclamation from the council: "Celestine is the new Paul. Cyril is the new Paul. Celestine is the guardian of the faith. Celestine agrees with the council. There is one Celestine, one Cyril, one faith of the council, one faith of the worldwide church."

Rome not only fell heir to all of the accumulated Eastern doctrine but, more importantly, it inherited Cyril's masterpiece: the dismembered and confounded Gospel of Jesus, plus additions. We call it the New Testament.

That doesn't mean it was all smooth sailing ahead, though. Theodosius called another council at Ephesus in 449, which would become known as the Robber Synod. That meeting was conducted by Dioscorus, Cyril's successor as patriarch of Alexandria, who after one debate, summoned guards, a mob followed, and the synod ended in disarray. Reminiscent of the riot Cyril's thugs started in 431, Dioscorus' riot probably covered the theft of whatever the Egyptians didn't get the first time.

The upshot was that Theodosius broke with the pope and, blaming his empress and one of his ministers for the whole mess, he actually put them out onto the street.

In researching for this treatise, it first appeared that the Patriarch Cyril of Alexandria was the lone culprit, but it turned out to be more complicated. The 5th century scholar Jerome would have to be taken into account, along with Cyril's Uncle Theophilus.

Jerome, who is usually credited with translating both the Old and New Testaments into Latin (the famous Vulgate of the Roman Catholic Church), died in 420. That would mean he completed his translation at least 11 years before 431, the year of the Council of Ephesus.

While that isn't a large time gap, it is nevertheless a gap. The original conspiracy theory had Cyril stealing John's scroll from Ephesus in 431, giving the Egyptians a monopoly. Then, they could have prevented all others from making copies, have allowed the vandals to alter the manuscript and have distributed copies of the altered document. If Cyril were the sole culprit, Jerome would have had to make his translation AFTER the Council of 431.

Jerome supposedly was born to wealthy Christian parents in Dalmatia, went to Antioch where he stayed a long time, left to become a hermit, then returned to be ordained a priest. He studied in Constantinople under Gregory of Nazianzus, a father of the Eastern church, and eventually wound up in Rome where he became Pope Damasus' literary secretary.

Now Damasus, who reigned as bishop of Rome from 366 to 384, was really the first to make a case for Rome's primacy, based on the tradition that Peter had been in Rome 300 years before. Earlier bishops hadn't even made the claim and, even in the 4th and 5th centuries, the popes were more occupied with the various barbarian tribes than they were with details. Pope Celestine missed the Council of 431, for example, because the barbarians were threatening the very heart of the empire.

Jerome's big break came when Damasus commissioned him to create a Latin Old Testament from the oldest available Hebrew manuscripts, and a Latin New Testament from the oldest available Greek sources.

According to one account, he translated the gospels as early as 384, from an Old Latin version, but that can't be verified, and we're not sure what they might have looked like. We're pretty sure, however, that Jerome spent about 20 of his last 25 years in Bethlehem, traditional birthplace of Jesus, where he established a monastery and worked on his translation.

Translation was a mammoth job in itself, even without conducting a wide search for the oldest manuscripts. Compare Damasus' one-man gang to that of King James I, who put 47 distinguished scholars to work on the same task. Split among six teams at Oxford, Cambridge and Westminster, they produced the King James Bible in English.

If Jerome wanted an inspiring setting in which to work, he couldn't have chosen one better than Bethlehem. It was not, however, where one would expect to find the oldest Hebrew sources for the Old Testament.

Jerome is said, however, to have visited the famous library of Origen at Caesarea, about 60 miles from Bethlehem. Origen, often acknowledged to be the greatest teacher in the history of the church, once headed the school of Alexandria. One account says Jerome became enamoured with Origen's Hexapla, or six-fold Old Testament consisting of various Hebrew and Greek translations in side-by-side columns, one of them the Greek Septuagint.

While Jerome's Old Testament is an acknowleged masterpiece, translating from the Hexapla, the ultimate crib sheet, surely isn't what Damasus had in mind.

The Christian Bible (the New Testament including The Gospel) presented a much greater challenge for Jerome, because Bethlehem was the last place to hunt for New Testament sources. It is widely accepted that all of the parts that make up New Testament were written originally in Greek, not Hebrew or Aramaic, and few believe any originated in Palestine.

It is said that Jerome was the only Christian scholar of his time truly competent in both Hebrew and Greek. Although people who learn languages in such a vacuum usually do not reach high levels of proficiency, what he is supposed to have done is, nevertheless, theoretically possible.

But just how DID Jerome locate and obtain "the oldest existing Greek manuscripts available" and create a Latin New Testament without straying far from his monastic cell in Bethlehem?

Since the content of Jerome's version of the New Testament wasn't very different from the four oldest surviving Greek codices, which all come down to us from 4th and 5th century Alexandria, the question really is: Did he conduct a search at all, or did he merely Latinize the Alexandrian Greek translation – the final Alexandrian version. His version wasn't just similar; it was virtually identical to the Egyptian one. But where would Jerome get a copy of the Alexandrian version?

History tells us that Jerome had friends in all of the right places, the most interesting of whom was none other than the Patriarch Theophilus of Alexandria, co-conspirator in the rape of John's Gospel. Theophilus became patriarch in the 385, which happened to be the same year Jerome arrived in Bethlehem.

A closer examination of Jerome's biography shows that Jerome even took time off to help Theophilus and his sidekick Cyril at the Synod of the Oak in the year 403. That's where they set up a farcical trial to depose their chief rival, the good John Chrysostom, patriarch of Constantinople.

Theophilus and Jerome became close. They conducted a personal correspondence, and Jerome translated Theophilus' homilies into Latin. The two men also shared a hatred for Origenism, a "heresy" founded by Origen (185-254) who, like Theophilus, had headed the Alexandrian school. Both men earlier had been admirers of Origen, but they ended up turning against him because he supposedly questioned Jesus' divinity. Might Jerome's hostility have stemmed partly from his embarrassment over having had to crib from Origen's Hexapla?

Significantly, it was the Alexandrian school that gave us the New Testament. The canon, including the same 27 books as does today's King James Version, was closed in 327, in the second year of the reign of the Patriarch Athanasius. Playing around with the Bible definitely occurred during the long reign of Theophilus, but no doubt started even earlier, under Athanasius (297-373), who reigned 46 years and, therefore, also had plenty of opportunity. Even Origen (185-254) was rumored to have injected pagan philosophy into The Gospel, which is a stretch, but it shows that forgery was on people's minds at an early date.

Cyril didn't steal the Gospel scroll until 431, and the existence of Jerome shows that the rape of The Gospel started on somebody else's watch, not Cyril's. But Cyril's theft of John's scroll changed everything. It gave Alexandria a monopoly over it, not merely preferred access, as it obviously already enjoyed. With the scroll under lock and key, so to speak, Cyril and his successors and their imperial allies could concentrate on burning any remaining rival versions – as well as their own earlier versions.

The timing was perfect. Leaking the vandalized Gospel – now gospels – to Rome through Jerome gave the pope what he wanted and, at the same time, made certain that all of the Bibles in the West would match those in the East; that is, they would all be corrupted. And the common Bible would help to solidify the new alliance between Alexandria and Rome against the Eastern emperors and assorted Eastern "heretics."

The importance of the Council of 431 to Rome is illustrated by the fact that the walls of Pope Celestine's mausoleum were painted with scenes from the council. That is despite the fact that Celestine neither convened nor attended the council, nor was he even asked to approve the council's proceedings.

Afterward, Pope Leo I (440-61) strongly asserted the primacy of the popes, but Rome's ascendancy was rudely interrupted. In 476, the Eternal City fell to the barbarians.

Here, incidentally, is something for those who think character is really important:

Pope Damasus is said to have became pope in a hand-to-hand struggle between candidates that left 137 dead bodies strewn about a basilica. And church historians paint Jerome as a bigoted, ill-tempered, foul-mouthed man. While sharply criticizing fellow priests for living in luxury with "spiritual sisters," Jerome himself traveled to Palestine with a wealthy Roman patrician lady named Paula. We've already covered Theophilus and Cyril pretty well, don't you think?

22

AN ARAMAIC GOSPEL?

While we're at it, how can we be certain The Gospel, or part of it, wasn't written first in one of the languages of Jesus' native land – Aramaic or Hebrew – instead of Greek? There are those who like to think it was, although there isn't a single shred of papyrus to support that theory. So, what are the odds?

In the 1st century A.D., Greek was the lingua franca in the lands bordering the eastern Mediterranean. It would be surprising, since he came from just outside cosmopolitan Sepphoris, if Jesus himself didn't speak Greek. John the disciple came from the same place, and we know that John the Gospel writer, even if he wasn't the same man, lived in Greek Ionia.

There is another theory. The church historian Eusebius quotes the writer Papias of the early 2nd century as saying "the four gospels" were based on notes taken by Greek-speaking converts from gospel stories passed down orally by Aramaic speaking people. He said each of the note takers "interpreted them as best he could."

Later, we'll discuss the odds against Papias' claim (impossible). In the meantime, consider these two verses:

Mark V
41 And he took the damsel by the hand, and said unto
her, **Talitha cumi**; which is being interpreted, Damsel,
I say unto thee, Arise.

and

Mark XV
34 And at the ninth hour Jesus cried with a loud voice,
saying, **Eloi, Eloi, Lama sabachthani?** which is,
being interpreted, My God, My God, why hast thou
foresaken me?

In John I, there are these translations: "We have found **the Messias**, which is, being interpreted, the Christ," and "Thou art Simon the son of Jona: thou shalt be called **Cephas**, which is by interpretation, A stone." And so on, and so on.

If The Gospel were written originally in Aramaic or Hebrew, why would the meanings of Aramaic or Hebrew words have had to be explained?

WHY KING JAMES?

In order to follow many of the examples cited in this book, you should have at your elbow a copy of the King James Version of the New Testament.

Why King James? The best answer to that probably is "Why not?" There are other good translations, but none is more widely quoted, its language having the flavor of Elizabethan England – or was that Shakespearean England?

Everything always sounds a little better with an English accent, doesn't it?

23

BURNING THE BOOKS

I t is frustrating when history books are lost or burned, especially when they're lost or burned on purpose.

The case of the watershed years between 312 and 439 being "lost" from Sozomen's nine-volume history of the church is one example.

It is difficult to fathom that most of the books of antiquity were destroyed and, in the case of The Gospel, only a few small shreds of papyrus have survived. It's a lot like all of the dinosaurs supposerdly being wiped out 65 million years ago when a giant asteroid or comet struck the earth. Could a comparable cataclysm have destroyed all of the books of the ancient world?

The cataclysm was named man. In the early years of the Christian era, the angry forces of ignorance prevailed everywhere, and all of the world's great libraries were put to the torch, leaving only a scattering of books in private homes and places like convents.

It is recorded that as early as the 1st century Domitian was attempting to rebuild the empire's burned libraries, ordering a search for already-vanished books.

Scipio Africanus is blamed for burning the library at Carthage in 204 B.C. Several fires damaged the library of Alexandria, the greatest of antiquity, which once boasted more than 500,000 scrolls. About 200,000 scrolls from the also great library at Pergamum in Asia Minor, which dated from around 170 B.C., were grabbed by Marc Antony and given to Cleopatra to make up for those lost at Alexandria. Flames would destroy both the books sent to Alexandria and those left behind at Pergamum.

In the 3rd century A.D., the Heruli set fire to Hadrian's famous library in Athens and the Goths burned the one at Ephesus. The latter likely held the answers to many Christian questions. Flames also destroyed the Antioch library.

In the year 303 Emperor Diocletian ordered all Christian scriptures destroyed, just as Herod ordered the slaughter of the innocent children, hoping to kill the Christ child.

Rome never had a large public library, but its private collections met a fate similar to that of the others. It is said that by the middle of the 4th century, virtually no books were left in Rome.

A huge problem for posterity is that there were very few public libraries in antiquity. The ones at Alexandria and Athens were the first public facilities on record, and among the first to burn.

Christians were probably the greatest book burners of all. Bent on getting rid of pagan works and the works of Christian "heretics" at the same time, Christian mobs destroyed most of what was overlooked by the barbarians, incinerating their own writings in the process. The Patriarch Theophilus, for one, personally supervised the burning of the Serapeon library in Alexandria. Emperors both encouraged and ordered book-burning.

That atmosphere inspired a 3rd century Talmudic admonition that if fire threatened to consume the books of Jewish Christians, they should be allowed to burn, even the sacred names and "blank spaces" on the scrolls. Please remember this mention of blank spaces.

By the time an alarmed Constantius II decided in the middle of the 4th century to establish an imperial library at Constantinople to save what was left, it was too little and too late.

Early in the 5th century, an order from the Christian Emperor Theodosius the Great, to close all pagan temples, doomed most remaining libraries, since libraries tended to be attached to temples. The ones attached to palaces, needless to say, weren't safe from mobs, either. By destroying the pagan temples of North Africa, the gang at Alexandria contributed to the literary holocaust. The Alexandrians, after all, had rewritten the Christian Bible and were happy to see, and help with, the burning of earlier versions or competing works.

The final blow was administered by the Muslims, who overran Alexandria (in 641), Antioch, Athens, Jerusalem, Constantinople and the rest of the Eastern Mediterranean. By the 15th century, they had swept across North Africa into Spain, and through Asia Minor to the gates of Vienna. While Muslims deserve credit for preserving some of the writings of antiquity, they usually destroyed the Christian writings they found.

That's how the old books, like the dinosaurs, became extinct.

24

JOHN AND THE SCROLL

Let's backtrack a bit. For a thousand years the city of Ephesus had been a place of refuge where no man could be tracked down and captured, and whose temples were safe repositories – virtual banks for the Mediterranean world.

Among the city's safe havens was the Temple of Diana (Artemis), one of the legendary Seven Wonders of the ancient world; another was a temple dedicated to Serapis, the Roman/Egyptian god. Either of them, or any of several others, could have protected John's scroll initially, but eventually, especially after A.D. 360, when Theodosius I ordered all pagan temples closed down, the scroll would have had to be safeguarded elsewhere. Logically, it was placed in the Christian Temple of the Theotokos, or Church of John.

John's church had been built over his supposed grave on a hill at Ephesus. Those environs were appropriately called Theologos (Word of God); in other words, The Gospel. We know the area was called Theologos up to the Middle Ages, because coins found at that site are inscribed "Theologos." A domed mausoleum originally marked the grave; then, in the 4th century, a basilica was built to replace the mausoleum.

In the 6th century, the Emperor Justinian commissioned Isidore of Miletus, builder of the great church of Haghia Sophia in Constantinople, to replace the 4th century structure with one even more magnificent. Haghia Sophia, by the way, is widely regarded as the greatest man-made structure to survive from late antiquity.

From the beginning, Ephesus had been considered the capital of Christianity, which is demonstrated by the fact that pilgrims visited John's grave there up to the Middle Ages. They flocked there long after Constantinople, Antioch, Alexandria and Rome had become the principal centers of Christianity.

Cyril no doubt chose Ephesus to host the Council of 431 because of its association with John. While it cannot be proved abso-lutely conclusively, John's original manuscript almost surely was still in the city, and in John's church. It is the only way to explain succeeding events.

Everybody accepted the fact that John wrote The Gospel there — at least the individual "gospel" that bore his name. In a letter to the Council of 431, Pope Celestine wrote: "I exhort you, most blessed brethren, that only that love be looked to in which we surely must abide, according to the words of the Apostle John, whose remains you venerate by carrying them in procession." That revealed two things: that Celestine was convinced that the author John was the Apostle John, and that his remains were in Ephesus.

John's church in Theologos was known as the Church of the Theotokos, a Greek word meaning "container of God," undoubtedly because it contained God's Word.

Later, the appellation Theotokos was arrogated by Cyril and made to apply to Mary, who bore Jesus, because Cyril was campaigning to make Jesus a God and Mary the mother of God. That's how Theotokos came to apply both the John's church and to Mary's church at Ephesus, the latter being where the Council of 431 was held.

Naming an important church after an idea like Theotokos, instead of a person, was not unheard of during the early years of Christianity, as was the case of the Haghia Sophia in Constantinople and a number of other churches given the same name. Haghia Sophia, which has been further corrupted to St. Sophia, meant Divine Wisdom.

The fact that Ephesus was the traditional last home of Mary no doubt was an added plus when Cyril chose the city to host the Council of 431, since promoting Mary was high on his agenda.

Why was such attention paid to John, a mere mortal, a mere writer? In those days, great shrines were erected to gods, not writers. The Theotokos was built because John had authored The Gospel in Ephesus and the scroll was still there.

History tells us that when Cyril went to Ephesus, his people started riots. That was the perfect opportunity to seize John's manuscript (Matthew, Mark, Luke and John on one scroll), probably along with the First Epistle of John, and take it back to Egypt. We speculate about that epistle because it is written in the same style as The Gospel and in one of the patterns of The Gospel. The rest of the New Testament, including II John and III John, is not.

How about the Book of Revelation, which tradition says was written by John on the island of Patmos, near Ephesus? Since Revelation has defied human reason all of these centuries, it's really immaterial – except to some mystics and fire-and-brimstone preachers – whether or not John wrote it, or how the Egyptians ended up with it. Revelation is simply not understandable.

The Gospel is the issue here. We must admit that the riot-and-theft scenario cannot be proved absolutely, but such an assumption explains everything. And the probability is overwhelming. It explains why the four earliest surviving copies of the four gospels, on which all modern translations are based, all came from Egypt and all date from that time.

It also explains why, at that time, the makeup of the New Testament was frozen forever. Cyril possessed the original Gospel, and could refuse access to everybody. He already ruled the Christian world as nobody had done before or has done since, and he had the power to remake The Word – and his world – to his own specifications.

25

HOW TARES WERE SOWN

"If any man shall add unto these things, God shall add unto him the plagues that are written in this book..."

–The curse from Revelation

We've been talking a lot about tares sown among the words of God, and not all tares are the same. Some are relatively innocent.

Among the more innocent ones are the numbers placed in front of verses. They weren't in the original scroll. In most, but not all, cases they are logically placed and they usually identify where one verse ended and another began on the original scroll. The numbers, therefore, are helpful to the reader, and there's no reason to believe there was an ulterior motive for adding them.

Also, the earliest copies of the gospels that we have, dating from the 5th century, were not called Matthew, Mark, Luke and John. They weren't called anything, so those names obviously weren't on the original scroll. To name the "gospels" is certainly understandable; if you had four new puppies, you'd name them, too. But there aren't really four gospels, the names are tares, and the choices that were made are suspicious.

In most cases the motives for changes are completely evil. Sometimes counterfeit verses or passages are written and inserted, sometimes wording is changed and, occasionally, material is deleted. Verses often are placed out of order, moved elsewhere in the same chapter, moved to a different chapter or actually transported to one of the other columns or gospels. Most tares, however, are swaps, in which a verse or verses from one place is traded with a verse or verses from another place.

How did the holy vandals do all of those things without cutting holes in the scroll? They didn't exactly.

Papyrus came in two-layered rolls. On the outside, reeds were arranged vertically, so as to bend naturally while being rolled or unrolled. On the inside layer – the writing surface – the reeds ran in the opposite direction, horizontally, which provided strength. And the horizontal filaments provided natural lines for the writer to follow.

Unfortunately, the two-ply writing material made it easy for a vandal to make transpositions. He could simply peel off a verse or passage from one place and, with a little adhesive, switch it with a verse or passage peeled from another place. In the case of an older manuscript such as The Gospel, which was hundreds of years old when it was cut up, the process was comparatively easy. The dryness of age and rolling and unrolling already had caused the layers to separate.

What is remarkable and fortunate is that the vandals seldom destroyed text. They almost always chose to limit themselves to moving things around. Why? Forged material in new ink and different lettering would stand out like a sore thumb on a time-yellowed manuscript, as would blank patches where they didn't belong.

Another possible reason is that, regardless of what we may think of the vandals, they considered themselves Christians. Whenever they were tempted to be especially creative, they must have thought about the curse from Revelation, which led off this chapter:

"If any man shall add unto these things, God shall add unto him the plagues that are written in this book: and if any man shall take away from the words of the book of this prophecy, God shall take away his part out of the book of life, and out of the holy city, and from the things which are written in this book."

Even if the vandals weren't especially Christian, they were almost surely superstitious, as are people in any age.

The vandals were trying to destroy The Gospel's message, change its tone or meaning, water it down, or hide it. There probably was always an evil motive, although that motive may be somewhat blurred today, 1,500 years later.

One thing that we discover is that the vandals were concentrating on "improving" Luke. They apparently found Luke to be the least objectionable of the four gospels, and chose to tailor it – to make it justify all that they were planning to do.

The vandals wanted to claim that gospel as their own, so they forged a dedication in which they claimed the gospel of Luke came directly to the "most excellent Theophilus." Then they scrambled Luke. You may remember that Marcion of Sinop, 300 years before, adopted the same gospel, Luke, to rewrite.

In the process of rewriting, unfortunately, they also messed up the other three gospels, cannibalizing them for material to put into Luke, and using them to dump other material excised from Luke. Actually, we're probably lucky to have all four gospels today. It is easy to imagine the Alexandrians burning Matthew, Mark and John and publishing the tare-sown Luke by itself, but they didn't. Again, maybe the curse in Revelation made them hesitate. As happens today, people are always saving papers that later get them in trouble.

In a few cases, one is left to conclude that the evildoers didn't accomplish as much as they had hoped, lost interest and didn't bother changing things back. They keep us guessing.

In any case, The Gospel was stripped as auto thieves strip a car for its parts. It was savaged by a bunch of hateful, egotistical, selfserving, un-Christian vandals.

On the following page are listed some of their apparent motives. You can decide for yourself whether the changes inspired by such motives should be allowed to stand.

LEADING MOTIVES

- Turning Jesus into God, although Jesus said he was not.

- Elevating Mary to "Mother of God."

- Belittling all other women, starting with Mary Magdalene, whom The Gospel says Jesus loved.

- Sowing hatred for Jews, their prophets, religion and law.

- Minimizing John and his Gospel in order to set up an apostolic succession scheme based on Peter.

- Grafting the writings of Paul onto The Gospel of Jesus.

- Claiming that The Gospel was written by four men, in order to separate the four "books" and manipulate them individually.

- Attacking Jesus' commandment to love one another.

- Protecting the image of chief priests, sometimes even Hebrew chief priests, and attacking the idea that priests should embrace poverty.

- Making Judas the scapegoat – possibly partly on account of his name. Today, many regard him as the only "Jewish disciple." All of the disciples, of course, were Jewish.

26

ACTS, A MYSTERY STORY

The Gospel, when restored, ends with the crucifixion. We can accept or reject the epistles – all or separately – because they are ancillary, even unrelated to The Gospel. But what about The Acts of the Apostles?

Despite various claims, including one that it existed before Paul's epistles, the novel-like Acts obviously was a very late-bloomer. It had to have been written by someone in the Alexandrian school in an effort to continue the story past the crucifixion in The Gospel, to a better end.

Thus, Acts is like the first two chapters of Luke, which biblical scholars have always suspected were written by a forger to give the story a "better" beginning. Although acrostics and other tests confirm that the beginning of Luke is false, it's questionable on its face. Worse, it suspiciously parallels the story of the aforementioned Apollonius of Tyana, whose mother was reputed to be a mortal, and his father an Egyptian god.

Acts, which provides a conclusion to the Gospel story, is held by some scholars to have appeared early – first in Aramaic, which was one of the languages of Jesus. There is, indeed, an old extant copy of Acts in Aramaic, but it's a red herring. There's no indication whatsoever of any of the original scriptures being written in anything but Greek.

There are, however, two interesting aspects of that old Aramaic copy of Acts. The first is that the wording is almost identical to that of the 5th-century Greek manuscripts and, therefore, can be assumed to be like earlier Greek versions. The second is that the name Theophilus doesn't appear.

The Aramaic copy says: "The first letter I wrote you, O theologian, was about all the things our Lord Jesus did and taught."

Compare that to the King James Version: "The former treatise have I made, O Theophilus, of all that Jesus began both to do and teach." Theophilus was a theologian, but not all theologians are Theophilus!

If Theophilus wasn't in the Aramaic gospel, he wasn't in the earlier Greek (pre-5th century) copies, either, because the Aramaic translation was taken from the Greek, not vice versa. Unfortunately, after the Alexandrians "perfected" their "gospels," they did a thorough job of destroying all earlier versions. An earlier version of one or more of the gospels may yet surface, but it seems more unlikely with each passing century. Christians have been among the most efficient book burners the world has seen.

The idea that Acts could have been written in the 1st century was exploded by John Chrysostom, the most prominent doctor of the Greek church. He said that few in his day (around the year 400) were familiar either with Acts or its author, or even of the book's existence. He didn't get to say much more, because Theophilus destroyed him in 403. Earlier Alexandrians manufactured the Book of Acts, then Theophilus and Cyril, after stealing the Gospel scroll, cemented the two together to form the foundation of their church.

Cyril had several axes to grind, one being to belittle and denigrate Jews and Judaism, which he and his mentor Theophilus obviously hated, probably out of jealousy. And coming from the land of Isis, Osiris and Horus, where Christianity never really caught on with the native people, Cyril was intent on deifying Jesus and making Mary the Mother of God – like Isis and Horus.

The king of vandals must have been ambivalent about promoting Mary, since he, like Paul, had obvious contempt for women. What he did, however, actually made sense. Making Mary a creature of unattainable perfection provided a smoke screen for his continuing to snipe away at her flawed sisters on earth.

Cyril's biggest goal, however, was establishing that he and his fellow clergy were the successors of the apostles, with all of the power and attendant privileges.

Since Cyril and Paul shared the same objectives and gross prejudices, one might guess that Cyril or Theophilus authored Paul's letters. Some of the letters, however, were known before their time.

A better guess might be that some letters were written by Paul himself, if there was a Paul, some by Marcion of Sinop, and the rest by the Alexandrians. That would explain the many contradictions.

Did the holy vandals change Paul's earlier writings in the same way they changed The Gospel? That's a lead-pipe cinch, but it's unprovable; we can only imagine.

27

THE CHURCH ABOVE ALL

Today, we get this strange picture of the disciples. Almost immediately after the crucifixion, they are organizing churches, consecrating bishops, being consecrated as bishops and engaging in full-time nitpicking.

While we remember Jesus as saying: "…Thou art Peter, and upon this rock I will build my church," those words are a forgery authored by the same church-building vandals who sought to steal Jesus' thunder. Not being a Christian himself, but a Jew, Jesus might well have asked, "What are churches?" and "What are bishops?"

You'd think the first instinct of Jesus' followers would be to tell as many people as they could about Jesus' teachings, as soon as they could. Instead, their priorities seemed to be building shrines, creating dogma and setting up a hierarchical priesthood.

While the first churches gave a nod to Jesus' teachings, they concentrated on organization, dogma and discipline. The holy vandals' chief concern was not Jesus' words, either. It was primarily making the clergy indispensable by promoting the belief that the ordained clergy, and only the ordained clergy, had the miraculous powers of Jesus.

Forgeries inserted into The Gospel established that those powers were handed down by "the laying on of hands," from the apostles through the bishops to the priests, so only the clergy could administer the sacraments. And only they could properly interpret scripture, although that wasn't really an issue in the early years, because almost everyone was illiterate. The priests, if they knew the meaning of The Gospel themselves, didn't bother to enlighten the unwashed.

The Alexandrians solidified the clergy's claims to special power and privilege by promoting the doctrine of apostolic succession, a concept that did not gain a foothold until many years after Peter's time. Power supposedly passed from Jesus to Peter, to John, to Polycarp in the East, to a succession of bishops extending to Theophilus and Cyril. In the West, the line of succession was from Jesus to Peter to Clement, to a similar line of latter-day saints who inherited Jesus' mystical power and authority.

Yes, Jesus performed miracles, and maybe local ministers or priests can perform a miracle or two – the latter, maybe so, and maybe not. But Jesus wasn't putting on a traveling magic show, nor was he trying to cure a significant number of people of physical ailments; arguably he could have cured everyone, had he chosen. He performed miracles to illustrate his teachings, the main one being to "Love one another."

Although Jesus supposedly was their inspiration, the Christian clergy always have been occupied mainly with self-aggrandizement. The aforementioned Clement, for example, is known as saint, pope and "third successor to Peter." The evil Cyril was made a saint and accorded the titles of Pillar of Faith, Daring Lion, the Burnished Lamp and the Second Athanasius. Modern popes, heirs to "the shoes of the fisherman," are called Bishop of Rome, Vicar of Jesus Christ, Successor of St. Peter, Prince of the Apostles, Supreme Pontiff of the Universal Church, Patriarch of the West, Primate of Italy and Archbishop and Metropolitan of the Roman Province.

A man named Ignatius, who is said to have lived between the years 35 and 110, was supposedly the second or third successor to Peter as bishop of Antioch. He is regarded, therefore, as an authoritative voice of the early church. His view was that the church hierarchy (bishop, priests and deacons) was a mirror image of the heavenly hierarchy of

God, divine council and apostles. Ordinary people, Ignatius held, could gain eternal salvation only by obeisence to the clergy.

Pope Innocent III (1161-1216), self-styled vicar of Christ, claimed to be "between God and man, lower than God but higher than man, who judges all and is judged by no one." That paragon of wonderfulness dispatched crusaders to kill Christian heretics in Europe, then launched the infamous Fourth Crusade that sacked Constantinople, all but erasing Eastern Christianity.

Questions of virtue aside, in order for apostolic succession to be a valid claim, one would think that all of the bishops in the line of succession would have had to be hand-picked and consecrated by their annointed predecessors. Instead, in the early years bishops, at best, were elected like governors and mayors in today's America. At worst, they seized office by force.

Priests weren't always special, either; their role wasn't even defined until the end of the 4th century. But when that role finally WAS defined, it was perhaps a bit overdone. John Chrysostom declared that "priests should be more feared than rulers and kings, and more honored than parents" and that "they have been entrusted with a heavenly ministry, and have received a power which God has not granted to angels or to archangels." Priests are feared most because it is believed that they have the power to DENY salvation.

The importance of the doctrine of apostolic succession to the clergy is immeasurable. If anyone found out that it is possible to receive redemption just by reading the Bible and doing what Jesus said to do – without any guidance at all – a lot of bishops, priests and ministers would be out of work.

Invention of the printing press in the Middle Ages threw a scare into the clergy, and the church in Rome reacted by telling its flock that they shouldn't read the Bible at all – that they needed somebody to interpret it for them AND intercede for them. Other churches have followed that example. Truly, many who read the Alexandrians' creative, but confusing handiwork, which has become our "modern" Bible, become so confused that they have to turn to the clergy for help.

From the Christian apologist Tertullian (155-225), we learn just how jealously the clergy guarded scriptures from the unanointed, thus guaranteeing the clergy's authority and future. Of the unanointed, whom he called heretics, Tertullian said:

"...we oppose to them this step above all others, of not admitting them to any discussion of the scriptures. If in these lie their resources, before they can use them, it ought to be clearly seen to whom belongs the possession of the scriptures, that none may be admitted to the use thereof who has no title at all to the privilege."

Tertullian emphasized the importance of slapping down anyone who would falsely lay claim to apostolic succession:

"...Let them produce the original records of their churches; let them unfold the roll of their bishops, running down in due succession from the beginning in such a manner that (their first bishop) shall be able to show for his ordainer and predecessor some one of the apostles or of apostolic men – a man, moreover, who continued steadfast with the apostles.

"For this is the manner in which the apostolic churches transmit their registers: as the church of Smyrna, which records that Polycarp was placed therein by John; as also the church of Rome, which makes Clement to have been ordained in like manner by Peter. In exactly the same way the other churches likewise exhibit (their several worthies), whom, as having been appointed to their episcopal places by apostles, they regard as transmitters of the apostolic seed. Let the heretics contrive something of the same kind."

(NOTE: If Tertullian is quoted accurately, "contrive" is an interesting word choice. Also, the leaders of the early church applied the epithet "heretic" to just about anyone).

In order to achieve his ends, Cyril got his hands on the original of John's Gospel, which included, side-by-side, John, Luke, Mark and Matthew. That permitted him and his people to at least figuratively slit the scroll into four parts and change the parts to conform to their prejudices before recopying them individually. Since Cyril possessed the only manuscript, no one could prove that the "gospels" Cyril's men produced from it weren't faithful copies. Only a handful of people could have realized the extent of what Cyril had done.

The vandals wrote Theophilus into Luke (at the same time supplying that gospel with a bogus beginning), and concocted a fake ending to Mark. Those were the twin Trojan horses that tied The Gospel of Jesus to Paul's letters and Acts. They combined those unrelated ingredients in such a way that the reader was left to believe that Paul and his cronies and successors were endued with Godlike powers.

Readers were left to conclude that both Luke and Acts were written by Paul's alleged friend Luke (some claim Luke was merely Paul's follower), and that the two works were tantamount to Luke-Acts Vols. I and II.

The vandalism not only tied Paul securely to The Gospel of Jesus, but actually made it appear that the Pauline material preceded The Gospel, which is plainly untrue. In this way, Paul and the rest were made to seem more important than Jesus himself!

It is the Paul-centered version of Christianity that survived – not the Jesus-centered version – and it was passed from Alexandria to Rome and stayed there, because the Muslims soon would overrun Antioch, Constantinople and Alexandria. The following quote from Pope John Paul II is chosen, not to dispute the Holy Father, but to illustrate for readers the extent that Paul has replaced Jesus in most Christian churches:

"Once Jesus reveals himself to Saul on the road to Damascus, and once Paul opens his heart to receive the gift, the apostle himself then becomes the revelation. He is filled with Christ, so that he can say in the same letter: 'It is no longer I who live, but Christ who lives in me.' His whole life, all that he does, says and thinks, his body, mind, heart and soul, become the revelation of Jesus to the world." In other words, Paul becomes Jesus.

But unlike Jesus, Paul preached AGAINST the Ten Commandments and good works. He preached that faith and worship are more important than wisdom, and that good works are vanity, a view that predominates in many churches today.

To some of today's advocates of faith above good works, even Paul's words aren't strong enough. They are won't to quote Isaiah from the

Old Testament where it says "all our righteousnesses are as filthy rags..." They claim that includes good works.

If Jesus could be separated from Paul, would it then be possible to establish churches devoted entirely to the teachings of Jesus? Maybe there ought to be churches devoted to the teachings of Paul, too, but it makes absolutely no sense to try to put them together and call them Christian.

It would have been better had the Alexandrians limited themselves to glorifying and enriching the clergy, but they didn't. They harbored a number of horrible prejudices and ambitions and, by sowing tares, made it appear that, through Paul, the vandals had Jesus' blessing for their un-Christlike words and actions.

If you continue with this, you will see how all of the vandals' changes can be eliminated, restoring The Gospel to nearly as good as new.

28

ABOUT ORAL TRADITION

L et's not accuse today's Christian clergy of lying. That implies intent. Let's just say they have been misled, so they are, in turn, misleading us.

How do we know they are wrong in claiming that Jesus was merely an "oral tradition" for years following his crucifixion – while Paul was busy getting the church up and running? How can we be certain they are wrong in claiming that four men belatedly decided to put it all into writing and each wrote a gospel, all because Paul's churches needed a written record?

One needn't be a rocket scientist to see the holes in that scenario, but blind faith is, well, blinding.

As for oral tradition, you may recall the day your teacher demonstrated how rumors are born. The teacher asked one pupil to think of something, then whisper it to another, then have that person whisper it to a third person, and so on until everyone in the class had heard it. Remember? What the last student heard was TOTALLY different from what originally was said only moments before.

Now, try to recall the life of someone you knew maybe 20 years ago. That's what the "four gospel writers" supposedly did when they wrote in detail about Jesus' life – years after his death.

Now, write down everything you remember. The teacher will ask three other people who knew that person to do the same and, when you've finished, she'll compare your papers.

The teacher will read your papers and exclaim: "This is unbelievable! All four of you picked the same events, on the same days, recounted the details in identical order, and described them in almost the same words and style! Even the dialogue is almost the same! I'm sending all four of you to the principal's office – for cheating – for copying off one another's paper."

If four men had written the gospels of Matthew, Mark, Luke and John as we know them, they would have had to "cheat." The accounts are much too similar. The four would have had to sit together in the same room and compare their texts line by line. It is somewhat surprising, therefore, that hardly anyone believes they did that. To the contrary, hundreds of books are devoted to explaining the differences among the gospels and to comparing the personalities, objectives, viewpoints and writing styles of the four putative authors.

But while the "cheating" scenario is far more believable than the multiple-author scenario, it is impossible, too. That's because if three or four people had worked together in the same room, there would be many cases in which the wording of verses would be identical, not just nearly identical. Instead, just one verse – out of thousands of parallel verses – is identical in all three synoptics. It is: "Heaven and earth shall pass away, but my words shall not pass away."

Could the author have made it any more clear that he expected The Gospel to be resurrected? In repeating this lone verse three times in exactly the same words, the author might as well have underlined it and placed an exclamation point at the end!

Instead of collaboration among three or four men, what certainly occurred is that one person sat in a room, with or without a scribe, and penned four columns side-by-side on a single scroll. Later, the columns would be separated and named Matthew, Mark, Luke and John.

The odds against The Gospel having three, four or more authors are – lacking a truly adequate word – astronomical! No, that's not the word. The word is impossible!

It's probably a futile argument, however. Despite those odds, supposedly sober men still imagine that if enough monkeys are placed in front of enough typewriters, sooner or later, by chance, they'll replicate the Complete Works of Shakespeare – or the Bible.

Sure. And if enough auto parts stores and junk yards are dynamited, eventually the pieces will fall back to earth as a two-tone 1957 Chevrolet station wagon with plaid seat covers.

As for the monkeys, eventually one might accidentally write the words "Neither a borrower nor a lender be" or "Et tu, Brute," but a complete "Hamlet" or "Julius Caesar" would never emerge, even if every tree in the world were turned into pulp and every last gigabyte of computer memory were brought into play.

Because literacy is on the decline in America, it is understandable that few people have any real appreciation for writing. And for a people who also are embarrassingly short on reasoning and mathematical skills, it is understandable that they can't recognize impossible odds. That's why lotteries are so popular.

That's also why some people can believe that three or four men wrote the four gospels at different times, places and possibly in more than one language and still chose almost the same handful of events over Jesus' lifetime to write about, not just in the same style but, in three of the gospels, almost identical words.

Two verses in the gospel of John point to the impossibility of three or four authors making nearly identical choices.

The first is: "And many other signs truly did Jesus in the presence of his disciples, which are not written in this book…" The second is: "And there are also many other things which Jesus did, the which, if they should be written every one, I suppose that even the world itself could not contain the books that should be written." The latter is an exaggeration and, as it turns out, a forgery, but it speaks the truth.

At the risk of beating a dead horse to death, it is crucial to convince you that originally there was a single Gospel, in four parts, on a single scroll, not four separate gospels by four authors on four scrolls.

Here's one more way to look at it, and then we'll quit. Any reporter who has ever taken notes during a speech knows what a great number of words a person can speak in just an hour, let alone a lifetime. Anyone who has ever taught a class in news reporting knows that any 30 students will write 30 quite different stories after witnessing the same event or hearing the same speech only minutes before. That's because people see things differently from one another, they have unequal memories and note-taking skills, they don't agree on what is important, and they have different vocabularies and writing skills.

Then there's the ego factor. Who doesn't want to be different from other people – and better?

Modern reporters use tape recorders and shorthand and wind up with thousands of words to choose from. First-century reporters (gospel writers) would have heard thousands of words, too, but the tape recorder and ballpoint pen and shorthand tablet hadn't been invented. Not even paper, as we know it, existed. So, when the alleged four or five or 10 gospel writers got back to their offices, they had forgotten most of what they had heard and were lucky to have come away with even the gist of what was said.

Whoops! They didn't have any offices, and they weren't writers. Of the fabulous four, two supposedly were fishermen, and they allegedly didn't write down their impressions until years later.

At any rate, not even modern reporters with ballpoint pens, shorthand skills and reporter's notebooks can reconstruct an event or a speech word for word, nor could four gospel writers relying solely on their memory. It couldn't happen with even a simple communication like a short grocery list or a fast-food order – not years later. We're lucky to remember those even 20 minutes later.

Instead of a grocery list, imagine having to recall what Jesus said and did every day of his ministry, and trying to summarize it in a few pages. Imagine four gospel writers picking the exact same (redundancy intended) events on the exact same days, weeks, months and years and reporting them in almost exactly the same words and in the same manner.

O.K., if you're not convinced by now, we should give up. But now we need to discuss "Q".

29

CONSIDER THE SOURCE: 'Q'

By now, a few of you may be asking, "How about "Q"? That might be worth discussing here, because the concept of "Q" is an example of how even serious thinkers might fail to see the forest because of the trees. They might. You be the judge.

For those who don't already know, "Q" is a manuscript that is believed once to have existed, but no longer exists. It is like an invisible subatomic particle that has never been seen, but is inferred from the way other, visible particles behave, as though reacting to an invisible force.

Impressed by the huge number of very similar verses in Luke and Matthew, some modern scholars conclude that Luke and Matthew both copied material from a now-vanished document that they have designated as "Q", which stands for Quelle, the German word for source. They see "Q" as an early collection of Jesus' sayings, etc. – apparently more like a spare-parts bin than another gospel. In fact, some present-day scholars have gone so far as to try to reverse the perceived process by constructing a modern "Q" from bits and pieces they've gleaned from Luke and Matthew. And they've published it!

Other scholars are hedging their bets. They are some of the ones who previously believed that the "authors" of Luke and Matthew borrowed elements from Mark. They don't want to abandon that idea completely, so now they posit Mark as the first source and "Q" as the second.

O.K., that's all far from dumb, but when scholars hit on a promising theory, they too often quit trying. It ought to occur to someone that maybe, instead of being made up of parts of a lost document now known as "Q", Luke, Mark and Matthew ARE the source.

That master "Q," we suggest, is John's original scroll, which contained not only all three "synoptic gospels," but the gospel of John. It is the purpose of this treatise, as you know, to encourage thinking along those lines.

Any exercise in original thinking pays dividends, and the compilers and publishers of the modern "Q" find that when common elements in Luke and Matthew are correlated, some parts are left over. Those should be regarded as red flags. We now know that in most cases – not all – those leftovers are forgeries; in other cases they are simply misplaced. The leftovers will give the experts something to chew on for awhile, even if they're not yet ready to take the leap we're suggesting.

30

THE GNOSTICS

Like "Q," the "Gnostic gospels" are a challenge to New Testament scholars.

Although early Christians knew many of the stories in The Gospel, almost no one actually had seen The Gospel. That situation gave birth to what we call the Gnostics.

If any of the Gnostic writers had a peek at John's scroll, it would be surprising. It is obvious that most of them didn't. The pious among them took what they heard about The Gospel and wrote it down. Most, however, embroidered on what they had heard, resulting in such works as the Secret Book of John, the Gospel of Mary Magdalene, and the adventures of a young Jesus – the latter closely resembling Super-boy of the comics. There also was a Gospel of Thomas, supposedly written by a twin brother of Jesus.

Then, as today, suppression of the truth was a license for rumor mongers and liars. The Gnostics were like today's tabloid writers and the authors of unauthorized biographies. John was born 1,500 years too soon. Had he owned a printing press and been able to publish his Gospel in quantity, the Gnostics would never have happened, and neither would the Alexandria hack shop that cut up his scroll.

Some of the more serious gnostic writings that survive are held by some to be additional gospels – that is, in addition to Matthew, Mark, Luke and John. Doesn't it say in the Book of Luke: "Forasmuch as many have taken in hand to (write gospels)"? That's paraphrased, but that's what it means.

No one was disturbed more by the 4th-and 5th-century churchmen than the Gnostics, who wrote hundreds of books that fueled the bishops' bonfires. The bishops weren't sufficiently disturbed, however, to share John's scroll with the unwashed – with the "heretics."

While fragments of the apparently huge numbers of gnostic writings had been found previously, a discovery in 1945 at Nag Hammadi, Upper Egypt, help us to better understand the alarm of the church fathers. These weren't fragments. Inside an earthenware jar uncovered by a man interestingly named Muhammad Ali, were 52 texts, including 13 leather-bound papyrus books.

The jar contained such treasures as the Gospel of Thomas, Gospel of Philip, Gospel of the Egyptians, Gospel of Truth, Apocalypse of Peter, Letter of Peter to Philip, Secret Book of James and Apocalypse of Paul.

Anyone who seriously examines the gnostic writings will dismiss most, if not all of them, so why did the church fathers hate them so much? They hated them because they reflected every "heresy" the church faced.

Christianity wasn't born fully formed; it developed slowly over the centuries. Its dogmas were hammered out in church councils where the losers of the arguments often were anathematized, exiled or slain.

What Christianity has conveniently forgotten is what the arguments were about. Many of those on the losing side considered the crucifixion symbolic rather than literal, and Jesus a man rather than God. Others rejected the idea that death, suffering and other unpleasantness are the result of people's sins.

Whatever your viewpoint, the papyruses from Nag Hammadi are obviously far more important to Christians than the much-hyped Dead Sea Scrolls, but Christians have not been told much about them. Ignoring them is the modern churches' substitute for the bonfires of the early centuries. It is much more civilized than burning, but it is similarly effective.

31

JOHN, THE COMFORTER

It's surprising what people believe, or want to believe. Some want to believe in angels, some in astrology, some in prophets, some in magic.

It's also surprising what people don't believe. For example, it's obvious that, despite their protestations, a large percentage of people don't truly believe in God, not any god. They probably are unable to believe – despite overwhelming evidence to the contrary – because they don't fully appreciate the marvels the rest of us see, and because they can't imagine an intelligence greater than their own.

On the latter score, few of us can fathom even a mortal such as Albert Einstein. We didn't appreciate Einstein's genius until the end of World War II. It took dropping two atomic bombs on Japan to convince us that he knew something important. Now we have that scientist's brain in a jar and stare at it in wonder, but without understanding.

There have been people who could memorize telephone books or see stars in the daytime, but few believed that they could. Most of us can't fathom the higher intelligence or abilities of fellow men and women, let alone the intelligence of God.

There is a school that says man doesn't do much of anything on his own. According to that school, Einsteins don't happen until God, the master intellect, decides man has a need to know. That's an extreme view, although anyone who is absolutely certain that God NEVER enters into the affairs of men is extreme, too. He probably hasn't given it much thought.

The premise here is that Jesus sent a "comforter" to us in the person of John, who wrote The Gospel. Jesus said he would. John was a giant intellect, an Einstein, if you will. Why not believe that God chose John to reveal to us his truth, and gave him special abilities that none of us can fully understand, because of our own limited mental abilities?

And is it impossible to believe that God chose an obscure 20th century American – The Illuminator – to be a latter-day comforter by resurrecting his word?

Let's face it, few of us will ever understand how Einstein, a one-time patent office examiner, figured out some of God's schemes, nor will we understand either John or our 20th century genius.

We like to say, "With God, all things are possible," but why don't we believe it?

32

OUT OF AFRICA

The sudden appearance of the four uncials today, after 400 years, would be like the complete works of Shakespeare materializing, for the first time, next Tuesday.

When the holy vandals finished their work, they had a New Testament that was pretty much the one we know today, only in Greek, the language of Egypt's rulers in the 4th and 5th centuries. The King James Version, and all other "modern" translations, depended heavily on the earliest manuscripts available at the time, all of which were either Egyptian or adaptations of the Egyptian model.

All of today's oldest Bible manuscripts are believed to have come from Egypt. They are Codex Sinaiticus, Codex Vaticanus, Codex Alexandrinus and Codex Ephraemi, and all four include both the Old and New Testaments. It has long been supposed that three of those manuscripts were produced in the 5th century and the other in the 4th or 5th. Those estimates appear to be right on the mark. It now seems certain that all four were made in the very late 4th or early 5th centuries during the reigns of Theophilus and Cyril.

Isn't it extraordinary that all four of the earliest manuscripts of The Gospel to survive were made at the same time, and at such a late date – ABOUT 400 YEARS AFTER THE GOSPEL WAS WRITTEN?

Isn't it even more surprising that, except for those four amazing documents, only a few sad fragments of "individual" gospels dating from before that time have been found? For comparison, Shakespeare lived 400 years before our time. The sudden appearance of the four uncials after 400 years would be like the complete works of Shakespeare materializing suddenly, for the first time, next Tuesday.

Isn't it interesting that even after 400 years, the Egyptians hadn't yet begun to call the "four gospels" Matthew, Mark, Luke and John?

And don't you find it interesting that, around the time the uncials were made, Cyril was engaged in a dispute with Nestorius, chief bishop of the Eastern Roman Empire, over whether The Gospel was one book or four?

It was Nestorius who claimed The Gospel was one, not four. It was also Nestorius who preached that Jesus was a man, not God, which would make Mary the mother of Jesus, not Mother of God. So he was exiled to Upper Egypt at Cyril's instigation.

Nestorius couldn't prove that he was right because he had completely lost access to The Gospel scroll. The reason for the 400-year gap between the writing of The Gospel and the creation of the Alexandrian codices is that the scroll was kept in a secure place where it could not be routinely handled. It is obvious that it was difficult, if not impossible, for anyone to copy any part of the scroll, let alone make a complete copy of all four gospels. Then Cyril stole the scroll.

While surviving fragments prove that "individual" gospels were in circulation in Egypt before the year 200, there are no signs that anyone was able to make copies of the whole manuscript (Matthew, Mark, Luke and John on the same scroll). Then, after Cyril stole The Gospel at the Council of 431, the Egyptians could copy anything they wanted without sharing it with others. That is, they didn't share it until after they changed it to suit themselves.

History says Constantine (280-337), the first Christian emperor, intended to make 50 copies of "the Bible" on animal skins for distribution to the churches of Constantinople. In those days, the Bible normally meant the Old Testament, although The Gospel might have been included. Indeed, the emperor and his bishop no doubt could have had access to the original scroll, if they wanted access.

Fifty would have been a lot of copies for those days before printing, and the churches that received them would have jealously guarded them, copied them and hidden them from enemies. Yet, not one is known to survive – not a single shred of one. So, it is safe to discount the Constantine story. As they say, the road to Hell is paved with good intentions, and Constantine just didn't get the job done.

33

HOW JESUS BECAME GOD

Amazingly, despite interference from the emperors and their puppet patriarchs, the church at Alexandria, not the imperial church at Constantinople, managed to hold sway over Christianity. Cyril, who was patriarch of Alexandria (403?-444), was only one of a long line of like-thinking church figures produced by the Didascaleion, the famed catechetical school of Alexandria. Many were giants, such as Origen, Clement and Athanasius.

In 367, Athanasius declared the final canon of the New Testament. It is significant that Athanasius' canon – which included the same 27 books that are contained in the King James Version – was closed by the Egyptians in 397. That was only 34 years before the momentous church council at Ephesus. The Egyptians were almost ready "to go to press" with their tare-sown edition of the Bible, and all they needed was for Cyril to steal the scroll from Ephesus and hide or destroy it.

It is not impossible that the Egyptians could have had a head start. That is because Alexandria was home to the greatest library of antiquity, which originally was housed in the Mouseion, the ancient seat of the Alexandrian university, where the early churchmen learned grammar, logic and rhetoric. If John had made an insurance copy, the most logical place for safekeeping it would have been Alexandria.

Alexandria's incomparable library once boasted as many as 700,000 manuscripts – Greek, Hebrew, Persian, Indian. It was, however, more than once damaged by fire. The Temple of Serapis, which at first had served as an overflow for the great library, then had become the main repository, was lost, too – deliberately burned.

History implicates Theophilus in the burning of the Temple of Serapis in A.D. 391, and that raises suspicion that he either was trying to destroy a second copy of the scroll, which he had been misusing, or that he was trying cover his theft of that scroll. Stealing the Ephesian scroll would have completed the Egyptian coup.

It's worth considering.

Cyril and Theophilus could do all that they did because they had become the most powerful Christians who ever lived. The two had bewitched the Emperors Theodosius I, Arcadius and Theodosius II – ineffectual father, son and grandson, who gave them permission to destroy the temples of other religions, including that of Serapis, books and all, and the power to banish their adversaries, among them Chrysostom and Nestorius.

Eusebius tells us that the Byzantine emperors were absolute monarchs and the vicars of God on earth. Yet, Theophilus and Cyril intimidated three of them, and dictated to them.

Theophilus and Cyril had an ally in Celestine I, the bishop of Rome. Celestine was either a true believer in the Egyptian brand of Christianity, or was impressed by how easily the Egyptians were able to handle the Byzantine emperors and the likes of Chrysostom and Nestorius. Whichever was true, two centuries later, after Islam had conquered Antioch, Jerusalem, Alexandria and Constantinople, leaving only Rome in Christian hands, the Egyptian-inspired trinity of father, mother and son took refuge in Rome, where it resides to this day. Father, son and Holy Ghost, another Egyptian-inspired trinity, also traveled West.

Did the bishops of Alexandria have access to John's original Gospel? They definitely did in Ephesus – and maybe even in Alexandria – as did a very few others in the four centuries after it was written. We know some separate "gospels," at least portions, were produced in the early centuries, because tiny fragments have been found – all in Egypt. Obviously, a few individuals were allowed to examine the scroll, but not copy it word for word, hence the "Gospel of Thomas" and other works that are, in the main, obvious paraphrasing and embroidery of the original.

It is doubtful, however, that anyone was granted an opportunity to copy the entire scroll which, again, displayed John, Luke, Mark and Matthew in side-by-side columns. First, that would have been a daunting task. Second, even if copying were permitted, because the columns were so repetitious, it probably wouldn't have seemed worthwhile to expend the effort required to transcribe all four columns to another bulky, unwieldy scroll.

So, in the 1,500 years since the original scroll was hidden or destroyed, no one has been able to imagine how it appeared. Not until now. Even if someone had imagined, he couldn't have guessed why anyone would have bothered to repeat most of the story three or four times. Not until now. Although many have doubted that the "four gospels" were written by four men named Matthew, Mark, Luke and John, that is about as far as it has gone. We are indebted, however, to Tatian, a 2nd century Christian apologist who had to have seen the original Gospel. We can thank him for telling us at least that the gospels numbered four – not two, three, five or dozens, as some scholars suggest.

What Tatian did with the "four gospels," however, proves that he didn't see the whole picture, either. Liking all "four gospels," Tatian combined them into one. The result, a book we call The Diatessaron, was used in the Syrian and Armenian churches for centuries.

After Cyril grabbed the scroll, however, no one outside perhaps a handful of people in the Alexandrian school would ever see it again – not in its original form, with the four gospels in side-by-side columns. And the separated columns never again would be seen without the Pauline writings and the rest of the material that makes up what we know as the New Testament.

We have no evidence that any complete copies of the unaltered four-fold Gospel ever were made but, if they were, Cyril and Theophilus, both famous book burners, no doubt destroyed them to protect their "copyright" by fiat.

With their cunning, the Alexandrian gang managed to defeat all of their rivals and to bury Jesus under a mountain of disinformation and myth. And under the influence of Paul, the Alexandrians smote the Jews and their rabbis, placed the Christian clergy on golden thrones and put women "in their place," as they saw that to be.

Bad enough? Yes, but then the Alexandrians went much too far. In the ultimate act of arrogance, they made Jesus God – even though Jesus said plainly that he WAS NOT God! Kicking Jesus upstairs cleared the way for Paul and his evil successors. As a bonus, that made Mary "Mother of God," creating a sort-of alternative trinity, a nod to the Egyptian bishops' constituents.

If we take Jesus at his word, that he was not God, then who can we say Jesus was? The Gospel also tells us that clearly. It says God is a spirit. Since that doesn't bother us, then why – when The Gospel says Jesus was the son of God, meaning he also was a spirit – why should THAT bother us? Wasn't Jesus' crucifixion, then, a spiritual death rather than a physical death? Wasn't his resurrection, likewise, spiritual, instead of physical?

Those are questions for individuals to decide, but one thing is clear as a bell: The truth (personified in Jesus) may be brutalized and slain (crucified), but it will return to life (be resurrected).

34

ADDITIONS DON'T ADD UP

We're just about ready to look at some of the patterns that were used in writing The Gospel. Understanding the patterns allows us to reconstruct the original.

Let's first take a look at a few examples that don't require an understanding of the patterns. They are passages in the King James Version that DIDN'T appear in the same places in the earliest Egyptian manuscripts. They are, therefore, either forgeries, or misplaced.

It's fun to try to get into the minds of those holy vandals. Can you guess why they would have wanted to add the following, which are in the Bible handed down to us from the Egyptians, but were not in earlier Egyptian manuscripts?

MATTHEW XII, 47: "The one said to him, Behold, thy mother and thy brethren…"

MATTHEW XVIII, 11: "For the Son of man is come to save that which was lost"

MATTHEW XXIII, 14: "Woe unto you, scribes and Pharisees, hypocrites! for ye devour widows' houses, and for a pretence make long prayer; therefore ye shall receive the greater damnation"

LUKE XXIII, 24: "Father forgive them; for they know not what they do"

JOHN VII, 53-VIII, 11: "And the scribes and Pharisees brought unto him a woman taken in adultery…"

MARK XI, 26: "But if ye do not forgive, neither will your Father which is in heaven forgive your trespasses"

MARK XVI, 9-20: (In part) "Go ye into all the world, and preach the gospel to every creature. He that believeth and is baptized shall be saved; but he that believeth not shall be damned… In my name shall they cast out devils; they shall speak with new tongues; They shall take up serpents; and if they drink any deadly thing it shall not hurt them; they shall lay hands on the sick, and they shall recover. So then after the Lord had spoken unto them, he was received up into heaven, and sat on the right hand of God."

Are you surprised? Later, we'll touch on most of the above, but let's talk about the last tare now.

Mark XVI, 9-20 was not included in early Alexandrian gospels but, more important, it is eliminated when the patterns John left us are applied. In restoring The Gospel, we must edit out some cherished verses and passages in order to resurrect the pure, distilled Word of God. Sometimes that is tough, because the vandals didn't lack imagination or writing ability.

Eusebius, however, didn't know about Mark XVI, 9-20, nor did Clement of Alexandria, nor did Origen, nor did Jerome. Even Sinaiticus and Vaticanus don't have the longer ending; they have only blank space at the end of Mark. Blank spaces on the original scroll invited creative writing.

Unfortunately, Mark XVI, 9-20 is the very foundation of many of today's churches, and it would be very difficult, if not impossible, for them to part with that fabrication. But John didn't write it, and Jesus didn't say it. Jesus doesn't need that kind of help, and certainly not from usurpers.

It would be surprising if the despoilers of The Gospel didn't make some effort to cover their tracks, and there is a hint of that. A presbyter named Ariston, said to have lived in the 1st century, could be such a red herring. One tradition says he wrote the longer ending of Mark.

We learn about Ariston third-hand, through Eusebius, who is often referred to as "The Father of Church History." Eusebius supposedly learned about Ariston through the writings of Papias, bishop of Hierapolis in Asia Minor and alleged "hearer of John and companion of Polycarp." Ariston supposedly was a kind of extra disciple – beyond the Twelve – who knew Jesus and told Papias about Jesus. Then Eusebius supposedly passed on what he learned about Papias many years after Papias' death.

All of that, of course, is hearsay in extreme and would not be admitted as testimony in any court.

35

PAUL A ONE-MAN TRINITY?

Could Marcion, Paul and the Alexandrians all have written under the name Paul?

Were you uncertain about the motives for some of the counterfeit or misplaced verses listed in the last chapter? That's understandable. For those of us who have grown up with those tares, and learned to rationalize and even to love some of them, it is difficult to imagine any ulterior motives. But the passages obviously were not in the original Gospel of Jesus, and how can that be good?

One must understand that forgery was rampant at the time. No document was safe from forgers because, in the days before printing presses, a book was normally one of a kind and, therefore, easy to alter. Even the great libraries, such as those at Alexandria and Pergamum, were filled with works that were elaborate mixtures of the genuine and the forged – veritable patchwork quilts. But librarians accepted even questionable manuscripts to keep them away from rivals.

Actually, the earliest books were not bound volumes as we know them, but were scrolls, as was John's Gospel. The more skillful literary vandals changed the meaning of a scroll manuscript by switching a passage from one part with a passage in another part, which created no suspicious holes.

The Gospel was an inviting target because it was made up of neat, short verses that were not numbered as they are today and were easy to transpose. Also, the scroll was designed with a lot of blank spaces, and the Alexandrians obligingly wrote in some of them. They had no idea that those spaces were traps, and someday would help in restoring the original.

Theoretically, there could have been more than one copy of John's original, but that would have been pretty unlikely, especially since The Gospel manuscript was exceedingly large and complex. But even if there was another copy, it wouldn't have been a problem for Theophilus or Cyril. History tells us that both men were avid book burners.

If we know that the Alexandrians DID make changes in The Gospel, we also might suspect that they made changes in the early books of Paul, or whoever he was.

It seems very likely that the 10 Pauline epistles accepted by (and perhaps written by) Marcion (c. 100-165), which lacked many passages found in our canonical works, constituted the complete works of Paul existing late in the 2nd century. Marcion listed Colossians, I and II Corinthians, Ephesians, Galatians, Philemon, Phillipeans, I and II Romans, and Thessalonians. Could someone in the catechetical school at Alexandria have written some of the other epistles credited to Paul? Could Paul be a trinity? Could he, Marcion and the Alexandrians all have written under the name of Paul?

And should we be surprised to discover that the earlier letters of Paul also have been altered to support the prejudices of the Alexandrians? No, that would explain a lot, but there's no way to know – not as we know about The Gospel. Fair or unfair, we have no choice but to blame or credit "Paul" for everything that is attributed to him.

Here's the question: How much should Paul matter to Christians? Shouldn't resurrecting Jesus be their chief concern?

36

DAMAGE REPORT

Were some people embarrassed when Copernicus figured out that the earth isn't the center of the the universe? Of course.

Did some people still refuse to admit the truth? Yes, including the church – for 500 years thereafter. In the minds of the Christian clergy, Copernicus and Galileo were purposely attacking the Bible.

But now that the scientific facts no longer can be denied, does that hurt Christianity? Not in the least. Didn't Jesus, who was the truth personified, say the truth will set you free?

It was a natural mistake for us to assume that the sun "rose" in the East and "set" in the West every day, instead of our little place on earth turning alternately toward, then away from the sun. The newspaper still carries the times of "sunrise" and "sunset." But does knowing the truth affect our Christian beliefs in any way? It shouldn't.

No ancient people fully understood the big picture. Ancient Japanese believed their islands rested on the back of a giant turtle, and that their ancestors came from the sun, but when the truth became known, it didn't hurt. Likewise, Christianity isn't going to be damaged, and the world isn't going to stop turning if we admit that The Gospel doesn't say everything it was intended to say. To the contrary. Like knowing about the sun, knowing about the Bible is going to help us to understand God's true design.

It all takes time, of course. A few years ago, lampblack and other grime deposited over the centuries was removed from Michelangelo's paintings in the Sistine Chapel in the Vatican. Art lovers had become so accustomed to the dirt, which had "softened" the ceiling's vivid colors, that they were outraged when it was removed. But our understanding of Michelangelo's work improved. Eventually, we'll get over our appreciation of the dirt, and we'll get over our appreciation of the tares, or weeds – a few of them strangely attractive – that have been sown among the words of God.

What would have happened had the truth become known a thousand years ago – that Cyril and his friends had muddied The Gospel, like time had muddied Michelangelo's paintings? Of course, that couldn't have happened, because the Egyptians possessed the only copy of the complete Gospel, John's original scroll, and were busily burning most of the excerpts that had been made.

But for the sake of argument, let's suppose our ancestors HAD managed to discover what had happened. Today, people STILL would be doing terrible things to their fellow man, but there would be an important difference. They couldn't use the Christian Bible to justify those deeds.

Let's see. We've already mentioned the Inquisition, the Crusades, the Holocaust, colonialism, slavery, the burning witches and books, and assorted other crimes and misdemeanors. There will be a lot more if we can't free Jesus' words from the tares that are strangling them. The truth will set us free, and no church and no Christian is going to be hurt in the process. A little embarrassment and the need for a few adjustments in thinking don't count.

Finally, the fundamentalists are right that every single word that Jesus uttered has important meaning. Make no mistake about that. But everything he said has a second meaning, as well, and sometimes it is possible to see others, depending mostly on one's knowledge of the Old Testament. The very complexity of The Gospel made it easy for the vandals to hide a few lies among the words of truth without being detected.

The tares proved to be parasitic. First, they fed off of the substance of the host. Then, for all intents and purposes, they took over the host. Fortunately, the same complex writing patterns that made it easy for the vandals to hide their lies in The Gospel eventually are going to bring the scoundrels' downfall.

In the meantime, it is comforting to find that the lies add up to a very small percentage of The Gospel itself. They are damned lies, however. While some were meant merely to distort or water down Jesus' words, others were obviously designed to destroy his most important teachings.

So, The Gospel needs to be fixed eventually, if it can be fixed.

And it can. That would be in everyone's interest.

Paul? We can't do much about Paul; the choice is to take him as he is, or leave him. But shouldn't we take into consideration that it was he and his followers who stole Christianity from Jesus?

SAME OLD CYRIL

A liturgy bearing Cyril's name is chanted during Lent and the month of Koyahk in the Coptic (Egyptian Christian) Church.

According to tradition, the liturgy had been given orally by St. Mark himself in the 1st century. It was supposedly memorized by bishops and priests and finally written down and "completed" by Cyril.

Does that sound a little familiar? As with The Gospel, Cyril showed no qualms about trying to improve the 400-year-old words of a disciple.

PART 2

THE PRINCIPAL PATTERNS

37

THE ULTIMATE PUZZLE

What was the original Gospel like?

In John's day, it must be remembered, the printing press hadn't been invented, nor had paper. Every new book was one of a kind, handlettered on a scroll of papyrus, a writing material made from reeds that grow best along the Nile River in Egypt.

By the 5th century, however, some books were really books in today's sense, that is, made up of pages bound together. Also, the pages were increasingly being made of parchment – dried animal skin – which first came into widespread use as a writing material in the 4th century. It is generally agreed that among surviving manuscripts, the four oldest copies of all "four gospels" were produced in book form in the late 4th and early 5th centuries. Inscribed on parchment leaves, all four are believed to have come from Egypt.

A book of bound pages, however, posed severe space limitations. In contrast, a scroll provided ample space, both vertically and horizontally, to accommodate the four parallel columns that corresponded to what we now know as Matthew, Mark, Luke and John. We can't know how long The Gospel scroll was – it depends a lot on how large the writing was – but some manuscripts are known to have exceeded 150 feet.

The Gospel's author was a master puzzle maker. The "four gospels" of Matthew, Mark, Luke and John did not exist separately. They were four narrow columns – like newspaper columns – on John's scroll. When restored to their proper places – using the patterns and clues left by John – the pieces form the outlines of crosses whose members can be read both from top to bottom in any one column and back and forth across two, three and sometimes four columns – from one gospel, to the next, to the next.

John constructed the puzzle from events in the life of Jesus to confound almost anyone who would read it. Why would he feel he had to do that? He no doubt did it because he was familiar with the swarms of ancient forgers who inserted their own ideas into the manuscripts of others. They cut, patched, erased and wrote over manuscripts – both papyrus and parchment – to change meanings, to steal someone else's ideas or just to obtain writing materials.

The Gospel of Jesus the Christ posed such a temptation. One can even imagine that the writer intentionally tempted forgery, since he felt it was inevitable, anyway. Intentional or not, by making The Gospel easy to manipulate, the author actually controlled the damage. If the job had been more difficult, the vandals would have been forced to destroy more of the text.

At any rate, The Gospel was written in such a way that no matter what happened, some latter-day friends of Jesus might discover the planted clues and patterns and, with them, reconstruct the text. In other words, resurrect Christ by using the very cross on which he was crucified.

Today, we are certain that The Gospel originally was made up of individual words, sentences, verses, paragraphs, and a certain amount of punctuation, as probably was the rest of the New Testament. So, one of the great mysteries is why the oldest extant manuscripts (4th and 5th centuries) aren't like that. For all intents and purposes, they were encrypted; that is, written in code. If they were in English rather than Greek, they would look something like this:

WITHOUTHIMWASNOT
ANYTHINGMADETHAT
WASMADEINHIMWASLIFE

Try imagining a sea of uninterrupted uncials (capital letters) without any breaks whatsoever – no individual words, sentences, verses, paragraphs, or punctuation.

The four oldest extant copies of the New Testament, on which our modern New Testament is based directly and indirectly, originated in Egypt and all of them are as we have just described – uncials. The question is, "Why?"

Did the holy vandals use uncials to confound any of the unannointed who might desire to understand the Bible? (They often showed their contempt for the masses.) Or did they use them in an effort to cover their tracks after scrambling The Gospel?

While the virtual encryption perfectly suited the needs of the holy vandals, it didn't originate the style. Most of the earliest New Testament fragments that have been found also are written with uncials.

It is easy to imagine that the original intent was to protect the scriptures from the "riffraff" – even those who otherwise might have understood the parables. But the uncial presentation also could have been conceived to baffle enemies, especially Latin-speaking enemies (Romans), who might find Christians in possession of forbidden scripture.

Another downside of the uncials is that they made it impossible to spot the vandalism, let alone repair it. Ironically, it wasn't until the Greek of the Egyptian Bible was translated into Latin, and then into modern European languages, that it became possible to picture how The Gospel appeared in its original Greek.

The numbered verses we have in our modern New Testaments were determined by a French printer named Robert Estienne (Stephanus), who lived in the 16th century.

According to an apocrophal story, the printer was correcting the proofs of his New Testament as he rode his ass from Paris to Lyons.

Each time the ass stumbled, Estienne divided the text. We shouldn't make fun of him, however, because he used great common sense in dividing the whole into verses, then numbering them.

The numbers are certainly forgeries, but they are very helpful. When the restoration tools that John left us are applied, most of Estienne's educated guesses prove to be accurate (that is, as the author intended).

There is one problem that is nobody's fault. We are handicapped by our inability to show in the pages of a book some things that are very obvious when displayed on a continuous scroll – as was the original Gospel, with Matthew, Mark, Luke and John arranged side by side, and verses staggered in certain ways. That's too bad, because in a few cases, the verses actually form pictures.

We will, however, do our best, and promise that the manuscript in scroll form soon will be made available for display on a computer monitor and for printing out on a continuous roll of paper.

On the following page is a small sample of the restored scroll. John, which has no parallel verses in this example, was on the left of these. Except for being in English, from the King James Version and not in the original Greek, it will give you an idea how The Gospel once appeared.

Luke	Mark	Matthew

Luke XXI

29 And he spake to them a parable, Behold the fig tree, and all the trees; when they now shoot forth, ye see and know of your ownselves that summer is now nigh at hand

Mark XII

28 Now learn a parable of the fig tree; when her branch is yet tender, and putteth forth leaves, yet know that summer is near.

Matthew XXIV

Now learn a parable of the fig tree when its branch is tender, and putteth forth leave ye know that summer is nigh.

31 So likewise ye, when ye see these things come to pass, know ye that the kingdom of God is nigh at hand.

29 So ye in like manner, when ye shall see these things come to pass, know that it is nigh, even at the doors.

33 So likewise ye, When ye shall see all these things know that it is near, even at the doors.

38

THE CROSS

"Heaven and earth shall pass away, but my words shall not pass away"

In hundreds of cases there are similar verses in all three of the synoptic gospels, that is, in Luke, Mark and Matthew. In only one case in the King James Version, however, do the three share an absolutely identical verse, and it is the one above.

That fact, by the way, destroys the theory that there were multiple gospel writers and they copied off of each other. If that were the case, many of the verses would be identical in all three synoptics and, in some cases, in John. Instead, they're all slightly different, although not sufficiently different that three or four men could have written them.

Of all that John wrote, why did he choose the "heaven and earth" verse to so emphasize? Was he actually counting on US to see that the words of Jesus didn't pass away?

While you probably didn't realize it, in the preceding chapter, you saw the most important pattern John used in the hope of rendering Jesus' teachings vandalproof. The answer has been there all along, for almost 2,000 years, displayed inside, outside and on top most of the world's churches – a cross, Jesus' cross.

Using the cross to protect The Gospel was clever, but not too clever. It was sufficiently clever that enemies preoccupied with selfish interests would not catch on, but not so clever that someone from among Jesus' real followers wouldn't figure it out someday.

John penned The Gospel so that it could be read both horizontally and vertically. It turns out that The Gospel is a "giant cross-verse puzzle" – like a crossword puzzle with verses instead of single words. Whenever there are three practically identical verses, or complementary verses, one belongs in Matthew, one in Mark and the other in Luke; no two belong in the same gospel. John provides continuity for the other three gospels.

When all of the verses of Luke, Mark and Matthew are in their proper positions, they form crosses reminiscent of the ones on which Jesus and two thieves were crucified. The three side-by-side columns form the vertical members of the crosses and, when lined up as they were on the original scroll, the similarly worded, or complementary verses form the horizontal members.

Note that the crosses are like those displayed in Eastern Orthodox churches. That is, the horizontal members aren't at precise right angles with the vertical members, and slant slightly. The skew in The Gospel text comes from the fact that the verses, when restored to their original places, are staggered across the columns like this:

Luke
21 And he straitly charged
them, and commanded them
to tell no man that thing.

Mark
30 And he charged that
they should tell no man
of him.

Matthew
20 Then charged he his disciples
they should tell no man that he
was the Christ.

The highest verse always is meant to be read first.

Also like some Orthodox crosses, the Gospel-scroll crosses have more than one slanting member – most commonly three.

Whenever the text is undisturbed, or after a vandalized text has been restored, a perfect cross is visible. The Gospel then reads smoothly from top to bottom, and its "parallel" verses line up on a slant, either to the right or to the left.

Since that cross-correlation happens hundreds of times in The Gospel, no matter how you count, the pattern cannot be accidental. When the cross becomes visible, it is virtually 100 percent certain the text says what the author intended for it to say.

In the King James and other modern versions, when the pattern of the cross isn't apparent, that is a sign that the vandals have been at work. There may be a verse missing in one gospel, whose presence would complete a horizontal member of a cross, or there may be another verse missing, whose presence would complete an upright member of a cross. In other cases there may be an extra, leftover piece and, sure enough, it turns out to belong elsewhere.

Christian
crosses

Although the Roman-style cross is best known among Western Christians, there always have been many other styles. Among them is the cross of Constantine (right). The cross of the first Christian emperor consists of an X, or Greek chi, superimposed on a Greek rho and stands for Christ.

Other Orthodox crosses, like the Russian cross (left) include both right-angle and slanting transverse members.

The most common modus operandi, however, is flip-flopping verses within the same gospel, although sometimes material is taken from one of the gospels and swapped with material from another gospel. In all cases, the crisscross pattern is interrupted, changing the meaning but luckily showing us where vandalism has occurred.

Remember that in hundreds of cases there are nearly identical verses in Luke, Mark and Matthew. The forgers' usual practice was to take one of those verses from Luke and move it to Matthew, giving Matthew two of them, and leaving Luke with none. Mark usually kept its corresponding verse. The vandals appeared to be the most interested in shaping Luke to their needs.

If, for example, you suspect that a verse is missing (a sheep that has strayed from the flock), you hunt for it, find it, and return it to the fold. That causes two things to happen. First, the original meaning of the passage that "lost" the verse becomes clear and, second, the passage into which the vandals inserted the "lost" verse also makes more sense than before. Of course, sometimes several verses are involved in multiple transpositions.

It is by such transpositions, omissions or additions that the vandals tailored The Gospel to their own uses. But it is easy to spot their work by following the cross, even after 1,500 years.

The rewards are great. First, Jesus' truth is revealed and, second, the vandals are hoist by their own petards (Shakespeare's fancy way of saying blown up by their own bombs).

39

THE CORRECT ORDER

Most of us learned as children that the correct order of the gospels was Matthew, Mark, Luke and John, and you might expect them to have been in that order on the original scroll. They were, and they weren't.

On the scroll, John was on the left, Luke second, Mark third, and Matthew on the right, just the reverse of what we learned. When the scroll was read, however, it was read sometimes beginning with Matthew on the right and ending with John on the left – Matthew, Mark, Luke and John.

Actually, the columns didn't have names originally; they got them only after they were split apart. In discussing The Gospel, however, the names turn out to be helpful.

The similarities in Luke, Mark and Matthew always have been recognized and that's why they're called synoptic, a word that means the same point of view. Ironically, the so-called gospel of John, which bears the likely name of the author of the entire Gospel, is almost always considered apart from the rest.

But John DOES belong with the synoptics. When The Gospel is restored by following the patterns that the author gave us, we can see that not only does the John column contain some verses parallel to those in the "synoptics," it provides essential continuity for Luke, Mark and Matthew.

The original order of the four columns will become evident to you as you study the scroll.

40

REPETITION

Ingrained in all of us is the idea that repetition is undesirable. We hope that we don't slip up and tell someone the same story or joke twice. We hate to hear, "I've already heard it." And people bristle when someone asks a question a second or third time. They're liable to snap, "Don't ask me that again!" In elementary school, we learned multiplication tables and poems by rote, or repetition, and most of us hated it.

Repetition is important in advertising and music and the telling of jokes (we know the third repetition is the punchline). We may hate it, and we may question its effectiveness, but repetition always has been an important teaching tool.

Before the printing press and movable type were invented, repetition was essential. That's because, having the only book or scroll. the teacher would read from it, and the students would recite, or repeat aloud what they heard. After many repetitions, memory took over, and the students could recall what was in the book without further readings. The Koran, for example, is taught in that traditional way to this day.

Thus, when a verse is repeated practically word for word in Luke, Mark, Matthew, and sometimes John, the author of The Gospel is using the time-honored teaching method of repetition. It's not a mistake; John did it on purpose. And he knew that eventually it would help somebody recognizing the pattern of repetition to restore The Gospel.

41

PARAGRAPHS

Paragraphing doesn't have to be learned in school; it is natural for even beginning writers to write in paragraphs. You probably use paragraphs in letters to Aunt Martha. Logical paragraphing is the hallmark of good writing, and all serious writers either understand its importance, or their editors understand.

In a paragraph, unity is achieved when every sentence bears directly upon single subject or idea. When a writer departs from that single subject or idea, he forms a new paragraph, with a new idea or subject. It's not science, but it's close. Whenever unrelated material winds up in a paragraph, you know it, even if you're not conscious of paragraphing. It's pretty irritating, if not confusing.

John, the author of The Gospel, organized his sentences or verses into paragraphs, although the original divisions aren't indicated in the King James and other modern versions of the New Testament. That is because when the Egyptian vandals transferred The Gospel from scroll to book pages, they eliminated marks or spaces denoting paragraph breaks, just as they did in running together all of the sentences and verses.

With minimal effort, however, we can figure out where John's paragraphs began and ended. It has been helpful that a few publishers have recognized that The Gospel would be more readily understood if divided into paragraphs, and they have done a pretty good, common-sense job of recognizing the correct places for the breaks. But we'd better stick to King James here.

The reason paragraphs are especially important to us is that they help us to spot interruptions in the narrative. Those interruptions show us where the forgers inserted sentences or verses that DO NOT belong, or took away sentences or verses that DO belong. Once we know that, we can go looking for where extra verses came from, and return them to their proper spot or spots, or we can go looking elsewhere for our missing verses, and return them to their original place or places.

Then we can apply the previously discussed crisscross pattern to determine whether our placements are right or wrong.

42

VERSES

There shall be five in one house divided, three against two and two against three

–Luke XII

How's that for a clue? Whether or not John intended that as a clue, it is a perfect way to describe one of the major patterns he used in constructing Luke, Mark and Matthew.

In all three of those columns, or gospels, we see a pattern of two verses to a paragraph from the beginning to end of the restored scroll, with one exception. The first and last paragraphs of each of each chapter in the three synoptics contain three verses.

In John, the pattern is essentially reversed – three verses to a paragraph from the beginning to the end of the restored scroll, with no exceptions. Might that be John's way of telling us that the gospel of John is the alpha and omega – the beginning and end – of the other three? Could this also be his way of telling us he wrote all four "gospels"?

If interpreting the "house divided" passage this way taxes credibility, forget it, but discovery of the pattern brings the passage immediately to mind.

If you don't always see the verse pattern at first glance, remember that the vandals have made changes, and they disrupt the pattern in places. When the damage is repaired, however, perfect crosses emerge.

In dividing The Gospel into verses in the Middle Ages, Robert Estienne sometimes fell a little short of perfection, as you can see from the following example involving a three-verse paragraph in Matthew and its parallel two-verse paragraph in Luke:

Matthew XXIII

37 O Jerusalem, Jerusalem, thou that killest the prophets, and stonest them which are sent unto thee, how often would I have gathered thy children together, even as a hen gathereth her chickens under her wings, and ye would not.

38 Behold your house is left unto you desolate.
39 For I say unto you, Ye shall not see me henceforth, till ye shall say, Blessed is he that cometh in the name of the Lord.

Luke XIII

O Jerusalem, Jerusalem, thou that killest the prophets, and stonest them that are sent unto thee; how often would I have gathered thy children together, as a hen doth gather her brood under her wings, and ye would not.

Behold your house is left unto you desolate: and verily I say unto you, Ye shall not see me, until the time come when ye shall say, Blessed is he that cometh in the name of the Lord.

Since both paragraphs end chapters in synoptics, we know there should be three verses in each. You'll remember that the synoptic pattern is two verses to a paragraph except the first and last paragraphs in each chapter. That's why we know Verse 35 in Luke originally was two verses, the same as in Matthew. When the crisscross pattern is restored, it proves our suspicion was correct.

The example above is typical of mistakes Estienne made in numbering the verses, and they need to be corrected.

It should be added that while numbered verses and chapters are generally helpful in reconstructing The Gospel, they are not helpful in making side-by-side comparison of Matthew, Mark, Luke and John. The parallel verses were actually parallel on the original scroll but, thanks to the vandals, they seldom match up when the four books of the King James Version are displayed side by side.

43

SMOOTH FLOW

What happens most often is that the parallel verses in the three synoptic gospels are similar, even nearly identical. Occasionally, however, when they are not similar, they nevertheless complement each other perfectly. That is, the story line progresses from one column of the restored Gospel scroll to the next, to the next, in the same way that the story always progresses from top to bottom.

So please skip ahead briefly to Page 188. In this limited example, the story begins in Matthew, jumps to Mark, returns to Matthew, moves to Luke, back to Mark, and ends in Matthew where it began. Was John a clever man?

See how smoothly it reads from top to bottom? Such perfect continuity; a perfect fit, like a completed picture puzzle. We know that all of this can't be a coincidence, since it happens hundreds of times throughout The Gospel. That should be proof enough that all of the verses are in their correct positions, but another proof is the repeated key words in all three synoptics.

The final proof is that, when verses are in their proper places, they form the horizontal members of crosses, the cross being the primary pattern used by John in writing The Gospel. Unfortunately, book pages are totally inadequate for displaying the patterns, and only a few of the hundreds of examples, can be shown here. Remember, however, that the scroll is coming.

44

BLANK SPACES

It is interesting that a Talmudic admonition around the beginning of the 3rd century instructed that if Jewish Christian books just happened to be on fire, they should be allowed to burn – even the sacred names and the "blank spaces."

Blank spaces, which don't appear in modern translations of The Gospel, were glaringly apparent on the original scroll – with white space above, below, left and right of each verse and where the story was interrupted in any column(s).

Evidently, some blank spaces also were included in early copies of individual gospels, as copiers tried to imitate the format of John's original scroll, which had more blank space than space with writing on it. Blank space was The Gospel's unique trademark, and it's quite apparent on the restored scroll.

One can almost hear the harrumphing of the rabbis, who were no doubt scandalized by the apparent waste of expensive writing material. When they wrote, they felt constrained to use every square inch. What the rabbis didn't know was that the blank spaces were almost as important as the writing itself.

What happened is that the vandals wrote in the blank spaces. They did it all of the time, and it is an important pattern. The following idea is offered simply because the author is unable to rule it out; skepticism is certainly understandable.

John, who you will remember was an incomparable genius, made sure there were blank spaces near the passages most likely to be offensive to the enemies of Jesus – enemies like the Alexandrian gang. They could use the blank spaces to write in, without having to destroy any of John's words. As we have said, they probably feared the curse in Revelation.

Anticipating the vandals' actions would be super omniscience (if omniscience can be qualified) but forged words are inserted into blank space so many times that it causes one to wonder. Intentional or not, it worked out that way.

In the Sermon of the Mount, Jesus said: "If a man requires you to go a mile, go with him twain." Was John going that second mile with the vandals?

Did John have that much faith in The Gospel's eventual restoration? That's difficult to believe, but omniscience is omniscience.

The vandals, by the way, apparently hated the idea of going that second mile, just as they seemed to hate the idea of turning the other cheek. They disliked the idea so much that they expunged it from Luke, the book they arrogated to themselves. Significantly, it is one of only a few places where John's words have been lost. Fortunately, parallel verses in Mark and Matthew tell us where they belong in Luke.

The following example shows just how much space there was to write in sometimes:

Luke	Mark	Matthew

Matthew XIII

14 And in them is fulfilled the prophecy of Esaias, which saith, By hearing ye shall hear, and shall not understand; and seeing ye shall see and shall not perceive;

15 For this people's heart is waxed gross, and their ears are dull of hearing, and their eyes they have closed; lest at any time they should see with their eyes, and hear with their ears and should understand with their heart and should be converted, and I should heal them.

Mark IV

13 And he said unto them, Know ye not this **parable?** And how then will ye know all parables?

18 Hear ye therefore the parable of the **sower.**

Luke VIII

11 Now the parable is this: the seed is the **word** of God

14 The **sower** soweth the **word.**

19 When anyone heareth the **word** of the kingdom, and understandeth it not then cometh the wicked one and catcheth away that which was **sown** in his heart.

45

OTHER PATTERNS (INTERESTING, BUT OPTIONAL)

You might want to skip this chapter because, as your teachers used to say, it won't be on the test.

Including the chapter is risky, since if you're already inclined to be skeptical about the existence of patterns in The Gospel, the following might make you completely skeptical. Oh, well! It was probably too much to expect anyone to believe a genius like John could have existed, and that some latter-day genius could practically read his mind!

Described here are a number of subpatterns, probably better called clues, because they only appear sometimes. They helped our genius, The Illuminator (biography on Page 362), to reconstruct John's principal pattern, the cross.

Although helpful to him in his work, the subpatterns or clues are not absolutely necessary for your appreciation of the restored Gospel or to convince you that the restoration is correct. You only really need to know the basic pattern of the cross, the patterns governing verses and paragraphs, and the significance of repeated key words and phrases.

You may, however, find some of the following interesting:

Round about

Every time the words "round about" appear, the narrative is interrupted in one or two of the synoptic gospel columns in the scroll and is resumed in one or both of the other synoptics. This subpattern is useful in restoring portions of the synoptics where there aren't three parallel verses.

And it came to pass

The words "and it came to pass" also usually signal a change in pattern, context or order.

Chief priests, scribes and pharisees

We know how Jesus felt about chief priests, but his disapproval extended to scribes and pharisees, who were Hebrew clergy ("Woe unto you, scribes and pharisees!"). Wherever he mentioned chief priests, scribes or pharisees, John apparently thought the holy vandals would be tempted to put in their two cents worth, or otherwise change or water down the meaning.

Reverse wording

Sometimes wording in a verse in one gospel is reversed from the wording in a parallel verse in another gospel. This is distinct from the vandals' practice of reversing the order of whole verses. Reverse wording, too, often identifies spots where vandals might strike, and they usually did. For example:

> **Luke XI**
> 51 From the blood of Abel unto the blood of Zacharias, which perished **between the altar and the temple.**

and

Matthew XXIII
35 That upon you may come all the righteous blood
shed upon earth from the blood of righteous Abel unto
the blood of Zacharias son of Barachias, whom ye slew
between the temple and the altar.

The reversed wording in this case happens to point to a double
transposition.

Blank spaces

Mentioned before, John's use of blank spaces may have been his "going
the extra mile" with the vandals. He provided them with blank spaces,
saying in essence, "Write here," and they did.

Chronology

To anyone reading the New Testament today, chronology seems to be
generally lacking, but that wasn't always the case. When events seem
out of sequence in the King James Version, that is an important clue
that the text has been sabotaged. Today, when the text is restored, Jesus
travels in a continuous path; he doesn't hop around, back and forth,
constantly retracing his steps, like the March Hare. Also, time becomes
logical; sunset never comes before sunrise, and so forth. And as always,
when we get it right, the all-important crisscross pattern is restored.

Hidden numbers

This is the most sophisticated of the secondary patterns, or clues. Hidden
numbers weren't actual cardinal numbers; they were words suggesting
numbers, cleverly concealed in the body of text, and are an additional
means of identifying and eliminating tares.

Beginning Bible students may find the existence of these hidden
numbers unbelievable, but they have long been known to exist in the
Old Testament, and were well understood by the Hebrew priests. A

couple of easy-to-see examples of hidden numbers are included in Part 3 of this book, (Tare 27, Page 284).

Kings

The names of a rulers (who are above all, and therefore No. 1) are sometimes used to introduce chapters. Among them:

- Caesar Augustus in Verse 1` of Luke II
- Herod the tetrarch in Verse 1 of Luke III
- Nicodemus in Verse 1 of John III
- Tiberius in Verse 1 of John VI

Double-entendres and the Old Testament

In order to understand many of Jesus' double entendres, which are sometimes also clues to restoration, it is necessary to know what's in the Old Testament. Cross references to the Old Testament, included in the margins of some editions of the New Testament, are helpful.

AUTHOR'S NOTE

Critics are going to point out some historical and religious errors here. Indeed, this work is far from perfect, and I apologize, but at age 70, I've run out of time.

So, I anticipate attacks by Christian "lawyers," or nitpickers, a fate no doubt like being nibbled to death by ducks. But that's O.K.; the world need Pharisees, too. I only hope my errors don't cause the rest of you to reject the truth that also is contained herein – to throw out the babe with the bathwater, so to speak.

Isn't most biblical history debatable? And, in defense of historical speculation, isn't it way past time for some educated guesses about how and why The Gospel was macerated? For centuries, scholars have suspected a crime, but haven't found a smoking gun. We think we've found one.

More important, I am convinced that the keys to unraveling The Gospel, as described in Part 2 of this book, are beyond serious challenge. I think that when you begin to see the mathematical probabilities – when no pieces are missing from our completed Gospel picture puzzle – you'll agree that we're onto something.

If I'm wrong, it may be a sin, but the ultimate sin would be if the Bible never got fixed, and Jesus' enemies held him captive for another 1,500 years. This may be only the first step in a journey of a thousand miles – but it's a step, nonetheless.

Constructive criticism is welcome, because the Bible is sacred territory and should be zealously guarded. I didn't receive any tablets on any mountaintop. And, as we've said, this book is far from perfect.

What do I hope to accomplish? I have no argument with any church, or with Paul or with anyone else, not even Cyril at this late date. My goal is to resurrect the words of Jesus for the good of ALL Christians, as well as for the good of non-Christians who have suffered as a result of Jesus' words being twisted.

I have one other small wish. I hope that someday a few young people come to recognize that, even after 2,000 years, there exists no church based only on the teachings of Jesus, and want to start one that is. Would it be asking too much to have just one Christian church dedicated to the teachings of Christ, the founder of the feast?

46

WHO KNEW WHAT? (AND WHEN DID THEY KNOW IT?)

It's probably human nature to suppose that previous generations were less sophisticated than ours, but it's also a big mistake.

The philosophical discourses of the ancient Greeks ought to dispel that notion. The surviving writings of Cyril are sophisticated, and should erase any such ideas about that particular individual.

It is appropriate, therefore, to speculate whether the vandals might have recognized any of the principal patterns John used in writing The Gospel – that is, the cross, verse/paragraph and key-word patterns. After all, they had a great advantage over us. They were looking at John's actual scroll, with the four "gospels" displayed side-by-side. They also had a much better chance than we do today of recognizing some secondary patterns, such as the various transitional phrases like "round about" and "it came to pass," and guessing at the function of blank space.

We might like to think it unlikely that when chief priests, scribes and Pharisees were mentioned, that the vandals recognized that John had their number, but we can't be certain of that, either.

John's patterns certainly aren't obvious in today's Gospel format, and they weren't absolutely obvious to readers 1,500 years ago, either – not even with their advantage. But if the vandals did detect some patterns or subpatterns, it gave them extra incentive to slit apart the "gospels," give them names as though they had been written by four individuals, and deal with them separately.

It's your guess!

Now you're going to be asked to make another leap of imagination. Nobody's going to call you chicken if you choose not to jump again; you've shown admirable daring already. But we hope you'll look at just a few of the more easily understood examples of the vandals' work and how they can be undone.

Hopefully, you'll see that when all of the pieces are reassembled, and crosses appear out of the wreckage, we know with near mathematical certainty that we have solved John's puzzle. We are nearly as confident as we would be after finishing a jigsaw picture puzzle of the Eiffel Tower or Taj Mahal. The motives for butchering The Gospel are another matter. Your guesses are as good as anyone's, and maybe you'll have as much fun as we did.

The examples in Part 3 are among the less complicated ones – mostly simple forgeries, as opposed to transpositions. That is because the more complex tares, including double and triple transpositions, can't be shown adequately within the margins of book pages. A few examples toward the end are from moderately complex to very complex, but they won't be on the test. We promise.

You'll see that sometimes the culprits had big things in mind, and sometimes they were being just plain silly, for lack of a better word. Hopefully, though, you'll recognize that the combined effect of hundreds of changes, no matter how small, is to seriously pervert Jesus' message.

We knew from the beginning that we'd only be able to cover a few tares here. There are many other places where The Gospel has been tampered with, but multiple transpositions can be shown properly only on a scroll. All changes and restorations, for that matter, are better viewed on a scroll.

Especially frustrating is the inability to show those cases in which the author of The Gospel actually formed pictures with words – pictures that are too large for book pages. Among the pictures are trees, a large alpha and omega, a fish and a bent-over woman. When Jesus says, "Behold the fig tree, and all the trees," an outline of a large tree with branches, trunk and roots appears on the scroll.

In the greatly compressed "fig tree" on the next page – visible following restoration – verses from Matthew form the trunk, verses from Matthew, Mark and Luke form the branches and Matthew and Luke form the roots. There are other "trees," too – "sycamore and sycamine." And yes, all you nitpickers, they're all pretty much alike. Some people are REALLY hard to impress.

So, you can forget the pictures, if you want. We feel that when you see some of the samples contained in the next few pages, you won't need pictures but, if you ever DO see the scroll, we'll bet the hair on the back of your neck will stand up.

We hope we've whetted your appetite, because the entire four-fold Gospel has been resurrected in scroll format and copies soon will be available. Please excuse the commercial.

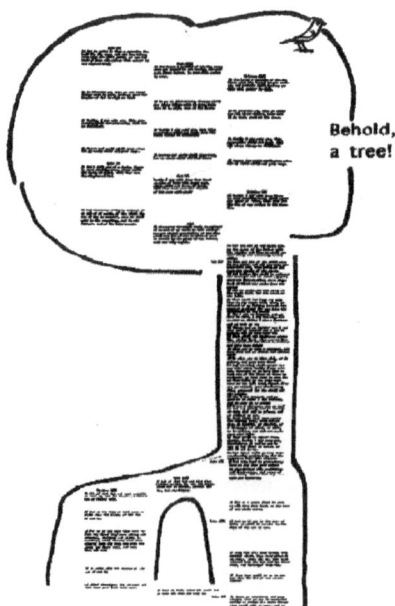

Behold, a tree!

PART 3

SELECTED TARES

A tare sampler

1

SMITING JEWS

The most egregious anti-Semitic passages in the New Testament are contained in the letters of Paul and the Book of Acts, not in The Gospel. Attached to Jesus' Gospel by the early church, all of those writings ideally should be detached.

Having said that, it is highly unlikely that the Paul/Jesus churches ever will change and, besides, many of those churches make positive contributions. They may as well be left alone; that is, as long as they don't revert to such nasty old habits as subjugating women, persecuting Jews, justifying slavery, and burning witches and books.

But for those who would be guided solely by Jesus' teachings, the inviolability of The Gospel is of the utmost importance. Although anti-Semitism in The Gospel is less virulent than that of Paul's letters and the Book of Acts, those places in The Gospel where Jesus' words have been twisted to appear to agree with Paul's bigotry need to be fixed now.

The worst thing the vandals did was to encourage persecution of Jews, and the following is an example:

According to Luke, 40 days after Jesus was born, his parents took him to Jerusalem to offer a sacrifice. But would they have visited the capital of Herod the Great if they had feared that the Hebrew king was a threat to the life of their child?

Was Herod a threat? Contrast Luke to the account in Matthew covering the days following Jesus' birth. Matthew says that, because they feared King Herod, Mary and Joseph fled with Jesus to Egypt.

THE CRIME: The 5th century Alexandrians concocted the story about the flight to Egypt.

POSSIBLE MOTIVES: Having Egypt shelter the holy family fleeing a death sentence (issued by a Jewish king), denigrates Israel and casts Egypt in a favorable light. By the way, Josephus, in his *Antiquities of the Jews,* doesn't mention the massacre of the innocents told about in The Gospel.

This is a paragraph in Luke II, as restored:

> 22 And when the days of her purification according to the law of Moses were accomplished, they brought him to Jerusalem, to present him to the Lord;
> 24 And to offer a sacrifice according to that which is said in the law of the Lord, a pair of turtle doves, or two young pigeons.
> 39 And when they had performed all things according to the law of the Lord, they returned into Galilee to their own city Nazareth.

The above example contains multiple tricks employed by the vandals. It is easy to see that 22 and 24 originally constituted one verse. So, naturally, you ask, what about Verse 23 in the King James Version? Let's look at 23:

> 23(As is written in the law of the Lord, Every male that openeth the womb shall be called holy to the Lord;)

Verse 23 obviously interrupts the flow between 22 and 24, and also interrupts the pattern of the cross, as there is no parallel to Verse 23 in either Mark or Matthew. So, Verse 23 must be considered a tare, and must be deleted – at least from this spot.

THE CRIME: Manufacturing a verse, splitting an authentic verse, and relocating another to counter text that the vandal(s) didn't like.

POSSIBLE MOTIVES: Anti-Semitism. Cyril and his friends, as did Paul, disliked the Jews, the Hebrew religion and the law of Moses (the Ten Commandments). The bogus Verse 23 placed in between real Verses 22 and 24 which, we have said, originally constituted a single verse, is an attack on the Commandments.

Cyril and his friends, like Paul, were in complete opposition to Jesus when it came to the Commandments. Yet, Jesus was crystal clear in his Sermon on the Mount: "Think not that I am come to destroy the law, or the prophets: I am not come to destroy, but to fulfill. For verily I say unto you, till heaven and earth pass, one jot or one tittle shall in no wise pass from the law, till all be fulfilled." He spoke of the law of the Jews, the Ten Commandments.

Incidentally, please note that bogus Verse 23 is enclosed in parentheses. Words in parentheses invariably interrupt John's patterns and turn out to be forgeries. Biblical scholars have long supected that this was so but couldn't prove it. In some cases, it is fairly likely that parenthetical matter started out as notes written in the margins of earlier manuscripts, and was simply inserted into the text during copying. In most cases, however, the additions are the result of evil intent.

Now that we know that "Verse 22-24" and Verse 39 originally made up a single two-verse paragraph in Luke, you may ask, "What about verses between 24 and 39?"

More than 90 percent of The Gospel came to us as written, although some elements have been moved around. Verses 25 through 38, however, are one of the few large-scale additions, or forgeries. They are devoted to Simeon and Anna, who supposedly encountered the holy family at the temple.

Simeon, described as a just and devout man, said the Holy Ghost told him that he "should not see death before he had seen the Lord's Christ." Anna, described as a prophetess, "gave thanks likewise unto the Lord."

THE CRIME: On the surface, it is a lengthy but harmless diversion, but it is, nevertheless, a forgery. It also is likely a subliminal advertisement for Peter.

POSSIBLE MOTIVES: Could it be only a coincidence that the old man's name was Simeon? Simeon (Simon) was also the other name of Peter, the apostle whom the Egyptians promoted to establish their church hierarchy. Apostolic succession was another major plank in the Egyptians' platform. Sure, choice of the name Simeon could be a coincidence, but he could have been given a hundred names other than Simeon. What are the odds?

2

SMITING JEWS

The holy vandals' hatred for the Jews and their religion is their undoing, because the intensity of their hatred makes their motives transparent. Take, for instance, Verse 24 in Luke XXI:

> **Luke XXI**
> 24 And they shall fall by the edge of the sword, and shall be led away captive into all nations; and Jerusalem shall be trodden down of the Gentiles until the times of the Gentiles be fulfilled.

This was the fond wish of both Cyril and Paul. The vandals wanted so badly to say this, exactly in this way, that they didn't even bother using any of their usual tricks. So they forged the "perfect" expression and inserted it. We are certain that it is a forgery because there is no companion verse in either Mark or Matthew, nor is there anywhere else in the other three gospels where it might restore continuity.

THE CRIME: Stirring up the rabble against the Jews and their religion.

POSSIBLE MOTIVES: Destruction of the Jews and their religion.

The Gospel contains many attempts to incite the rabble against the Jews, or at least put them in a bad light, and all are motivated at bottom by the idea that "the Jews" killed Jesus. Together with the Paulist writings, these have supplied Christians with an excuse for brutalizing Jews for 1,500 years.

Here is another example and, again, Luke has been used shamelessly:

Luke XXI
20 And when ye shall see Jerusalem encompassed with armies then know that the desolation thereof is nigh.
21 Then let them which are in Judea flee to the mountains; and let them which are in the midst of it depart out; and let not them that are in the countries enter thereinto.

Most of this was manufactured by the holy vandals, who would have liked to see Jerusalem surrounded by armies and its inhabitants punished, exiled, or killed. Some of today's preachers love these verses too much.

Compare the above corrupted version in Luke with the following parallel counterparts in the restored columns of Mark and Matthew, which mention neither Jerusalem nor armies:

Mark XIII
14 But when ye shall see the abomination of desolation, spoken of by Daniel the prophet standing where it ought not [...] then let them that be in Judea flee to the mountains: 18 And pray ye that your flight be not in winter.

Matthew XXIV
15 When ye therefore shall see the abomination of desolation spoken of by Daniel the prophet stand(ing) in the holy place [...]
16 Then let them which be in Judea flee into the

mountains. 20 But pray ye that your flight be not in winter, neither on the sabbath day.

Also, for some reason, the vandals tampered to a lesser degree with the parallel verses in Mark and Matthew. Where the ellipses wihin brackets appear in the restored verses above, they inserted "Let him that readeth understand" in Mark and "Whoso readeth, let him understand" in Matthew. But they weren't thinking straight, because Jesus was speaking, not writing. It was the vandals who were writing; they were writing on the original scroll. One would have to guess they were trying to call attention to their counterfeit "masterpiece" in Luke.

The evildoers were busy on this one. They also moved "And pray ye that your flight be not in winter" several verses lower in Mark, and moved "But pray ye that your flight be not in winter, neither on the sabbath day" lower in Matthew. Why? Who can fully understand the vandals' twisted minds? Regardless, restoring those verses to their proper places is worthwhile in itself.

3

PROMOTING PETER, SMITING JEWS

Again and again, the vandals sought to prop up the halo of Peter, prince of the apostles. The crowd in Alexandria evidently was bothered by what Peter said in Matthew XIX, 27, which was:

Matthew XIX
27 Then answered Peter and said unto him Behold we have forsaken all, and followed thee; what shall we have therefore?"

There's no ambiguity in that, is there? Peter, the man Jesus once called Satan, was plainly asking, "What's in it for us?" And that was enough to embarrass even the practically shameless Egyptian clergy, so they deleted "What shall we have therefore?" from both Mark and Luke, making them read simply:

Mark X
28 Then Peter began to say unto him, Lo we have left all and have followed thee.

Luke XVIII
28 Then Peter said, Lo we have left all and followed thee.

Proof that Peter's question originally appeared in all three of the synoptics is the fact that while Peter asks the question only in Matthew in the King James Version, Jesus answers the question in Mark and Luke, as well. Normally, one doesn't answer unasked questions.

The Alexandrians liked Jesus' answer even less than they liked Peter's question. In Mark and Matthew, where Jesus tells Peter that "many that are first shall be last, and the last first," they realized that Jesus' words could be construed as applying to Peter, who was the rock to which the church clung for legitimacy.

So the holy vandals removed those words, too, from Luke, the book that they arrogated to themselves. We know, however, that primarily for practical reasons – but probably for superstitious reasons as well – they almost always chose not to throw away words, but to stash them somewhere else, or trade them for less offending words.

So we go looking for the offending "first/last" phrase, and where do we find it? That fragment, we discover, was cleverly transferred to Luke XIII, 30 where it seems to imply that it is Abraham, Isaac and Jacob who could end up last, not Peter. The Jew-hating vandals no doubt preferred that scenario, but what Jesus said earlier in Luke XIII proves that he didn't mean Abraham, Isaac and Jacob could be last. He said:

28 There shall be weeping and gnashing of teeth, when ye shall see Abraham, and Isaac, and Jacob, and all the prophets, in the kingdom of God, and you yourselves thrust out.

When the "first/last" fragment is returned to its original position in the scroll, everything again conforms to the pattern of the cross, which means that's the way John wrote it.

THE CRIME: Taking embarrassing words out of Peter's mouth.

POSSIBLE MOTIVES: Making Peter look good at the expense of Hebrew patriarchs Abraham, Isaac and Jacob.

4

PROMOTING PETER,
SMITING JEWS

At John XIII, Verse 36, when Peter asks Jesus "Whither goest thou?" Jesus supposedly replies, "Whither I go, thou canst not follow me now; but thou shalt follow me afterwards." That verse, by breaking the crisscross pattern, is revealed as another forgery.

One should suspect that John XIII, Verse 36 is a forgery since at the Last Supper (John XIII, Verse 5), Jesus had said, "But now I go my way to him that sent me; and none of you asketh me, Whither goest thou?" And none of the disciples did.

But, at John XIII, Verse 33, Jesus tells them anyway: "Whither I go ye cannot come; so now I say to you, a new commandment I give unto you, that ye love one another."

According to the forgery at John XIII, Verse 36, however, Jesus appeared to be mistaken about no one asking where he was going. It claims that Peter did ask where and, apparently as his reward for asking, he was promised that he would be the exception. He would be allowed to follow Jesus later.

Two things are wrong: First, Jesus said not a single disciple had asked him and, second, Jesus appeared to answer Peter's question before Peter asked it.

The reason we're certain that John XIII, Verse 36 is a forgery is because it interrupts the crisscross pattern with which the scroll was constructed. It's a leftover piece in our jigsaw picture puzzle, so to speak. As usual, however, common sense adds to our confidence that the Gospel writer's patterns are a real and reliable guide to reconstruction.

THE CRIME: The forgery appears to give Peter a passport and a visa to follow Jesus, presumably to Heaven. The other disciples apparently must stay behind.

POSSIBLE MOTIVES: Having Peter follow Jesus into heaven is the ideal way for the Egyptians to start a church hierarchy. The hierarchy would extend from heaven to earth and down through the ages to Theophilus, Cyril and their successors forever.

5

PROMOTING PETER

Considering that the holy vandals wanted to claim to be Peter's successors, they had to do something drastic to eliminate or water down Matthew XVI, Verse 23, which says:

> 23 But he turned and said unto Peter, Get thee behind me, Satan; thou art an offence unto me for thou savourest not the things that be of God, but those that be of men.

So the vandals forged these three verses and inserted them ahead of Verse 23:

> 17 And Jesus answered and said unto him, Blessed art thou Simon Bar Jonah; for flesh and blood hath not revealed it unto thee, but my Father which is in heaven.
> 18 And I say also unto thee that thou art Peter, and upon this rock I will build my church, and the gates of hell shall not prevail against it.
> 19 And I will give unto thee the keys to the kingdom of heaven; and whatsoever thou shalt bind on earth shall

be bound in heaven, and whatsoever thou shalt loose on earth shall be loosed in heaven.

We know that the preceding three verses are forgeries because they have no parallels in Luke and Mark, they violate the pattern of the cross, they break the rule of two verses to a paragraph in the synoptics, and we can't find anyplace from which they possibly could have been taken.

THE CRIME: The vandals refused to let Jesus get away with saying Peter was offensive, that he savored earthly things more than heavenly things, and that he was, in a word, Satan. So they changed The Gospel, putting Peter in charge of heaven – kicking him upstairs – and, at the same time, installing him as the head of the church hierarchy back on earth.

POSSIBLE MOTIVES: If Peter has the keys to heaven, then his earthly successors, like Theophilus and Cyril, can say who gets into heaven and who doesn't.

Because of the importance of this tare, we will show you on the following pages how Matthew XVI, Verses 17-19, stand out like a sore thumb when parallel passages of Luke, Mark and Matthew from the King James Version are displayed side by side. The bogus verses are in boldface type. Note that Robert Estienne was inconsistent in Matthew, making two verses (15 and 16) out of what he made one verse in both Mark and Luke. So we combine 15 and 16.

Regrettably, book pages are not wide enough to display three or four columns side by side, so there is some overlap in many of the examples shown here.

Luke   Mark   Matthew

Luke

18 And it came to pass as he was alone praying, his disciples were with him: and he asked them, saying, Whom say the people that I am?

Mark

27 And Jesus went out, and his disciples, into the towns of Caesarea Philippi: and by the way he asked his disciples, saying unto them, Whom do men say that I am?

Matthew

13 When Jesus came into the coasts of Caesarea Philippi, he asked his disciples, saying, Whom do men say that I the Son of man am?

19 They answering said, John the Baptist; but some say, Elias; and others say, that one of the old prophets is risen again.

28 And they answered, John, the Baptist but some say Elias; and others, One of the prophets.

14 And they said, Some say that thou art John the Baptist: some, Elias; the others; Jeremias, or one of the prophets.

20 He said unto them, But whom do ye say that I am? Peter answering said, The Christ of God.

29 And he saith unto them, but whom say ye that I am? And Peter answereth and saith unto him, Thou art the Christ.

15 He saith unto them, But whom say ye that I am?
(16) And Simon Peter answered and said, Thou art the Christ, the son of the living God.

17 And Jesus answered and said unto him, Blessed art thou, Simon Bar-Jona; for flesh and blood hath not revealed it unto thee, but my father which is in heaven.
18 And I say also unto thee, That thou art Peter, and upon this rock I will build my church; and the gates of hell shall not prevail against it.
19 And I will give unto thee the keys of the kingdom of heaven; and whatsoever thou shalt bind on earth shall be bound in heaven; and whatsoever though shalt loose on earth shall be loosed in heaven.

21 And he straitly charged them, and commanded them to tell no man that thing.

30 And he charged them that they should tell no man of him.

20 Then charged he his disciples that they should tell no man that he was the Christ.

6

SMITING THE GOSPEL, PROMOTING PAUL

The mother of all tares, and the one that all but names the chief tare sower, is the first four verses of the "gospel of Luke" in the King James Version.

There are various reasons to suspect that those four verses are counterfeit. One reason is that there are no parallel verses in any of the other four gospels. Another red flag is the fact that four verses violate the pattern of three verses to a paragraph at the beginning and end of all chapters in the synoptics.

Immediately following those four verses, however, is a paragraph of three verses. So the second paragraph of Luke as we know it, consisting of three verses, undoubtedly was first in the original scroll, not the four verses in the King James Version. Incidentally, the beginning of the second paragraph in the KJV, "There was in the days of Herod," is a way the author often started chapters, and we will look at that a little later. But first, let's examine the four bogus verses:

Luke I
Forasmuch as many have taken in hand to set forth

in order a declaration of those things which are most surely believed among us,

2 Even as they delivered them unto us, which from the beginning were eyewitnesses, and ministers of the word;

3 It seemed good to me also, having had perfect understanding of all things from the very first, to write unto thee in order, most excellent Theophilus,

4 That thou mightest know the certainty of those things, wherein thou hast been instructed.

Again, common sense backs up what we know about the author's patterns. That prideful and ludicrous statement doesn't belong anywhere in Jesus' Gospel. No one even remotely connected with Jesus would have claimed perfection, since Jesus himself denied being perfect.

Verses 5, 6, and 7 constitute the original first paragraph of Luke, after which the two-verse-paragraph pattern should take over, as it does in all of the synoptics. (Frustration, frustration! The first two-verse paragraph following the three-verse paragraph at the beginning appears to have three verses in it. That's very untimely. It's one of a comparatively few instances where the 13th century Robert Estienne split a verse in two. Verses 8 and 9 should be combined into one. Read it and you'll agree.)

The "most excellent Theophilus" named in the tare at the beginning of Luke is also named in the first chapter, first verse of Acts, which begins: "The former treatise have I made, O Theophilus, of all that Jesus began both to do and teach..."

As you already know, in vandalizing The Gospel, the Egyptians concentrated on the book of Luke. They claimed Luke was written by a man named Luke, a friend of Paul who also wrote Acts, and that that gospel was received separately from the others. John, the real author, was not even mentioned, the forgery stating instead that "many have taken in hand" to write gospels.

With the Theophilus dedications in Acts and Luke, the forgers apparently wanted to convince readers that both books came directly to the 5th century patriarch of Alexandria, Egypt, of all people. And directly from Luke? It boggles the mind.

THE CRIME: The vandals, in effect, slit John's Gospel into four parts, then made many, many changes, with Luke being changed the most. They proceeded, then, to link Luke to Acts and, in essence, started a new religion based not so much on Jesus, but on Peter and Paul and an apostolic hierarchy.

POSSIBLE MOTIVES: The vandals were more interested in building a church and gaining power for themselves than they were interested in the teachings of Jesus, some of which they obviously didn't like very much. By putting their man Peter in heaven to head their hierarchy, and installing their man Paul as head of the earthly church, they could all but ignore Jesus.

7

PROMOTING PRIESTS, TRIVIALIZING THE HOLY GHOST

C lios is the name given to the statuettes awarded annually for outstanding advertising. If that award had been around 1,500 years ago, two phony verses placed in The Gospel then should have retired the Clios forever. That forgery, tantamount to an ad for priestly services, produced enough revenue to pay for all of the Bibles ever printed and all of the churches ever built.

It's still in the King James Version, inserted as Verses 22 and 23 in Chapter XX of the gospel of John, and it reads thus:

> **John XX**
> And when he had said this he breathed on them, and
> saith unto them, Receive ye the Holy Ghost;
> Whosesoever sins ye remit, they are remitted unto them;
> and whosesoever sins ye retain, they are retained.

If the vandals had only recognized the pattern of three verses to a paragraph in John, they might not have tried to get away with inserting that two-verse forgery. But they didn't see the big picture, making it easier for a restorer, who immediately searched for other places where the two verses might provide continuity. There was none.

POSSIBLE MOTIVES: That phony passage was tantamount to an advertisement for pardons. It is unlikely that Jesus intended for priests to have such powers, and it seems certain that he didn't intend for the clergy to sell them. Bishops and priests of all stripes have sought or accepted quid pro quo for pardoning sinners and granting indulgences. It could be said that those two fake verses set off the Protestant Reformation.

Whether or not money exchanged hands, those verses gave the clergy a power even greater than the power to forgive sins; it gave them the power NOT to forgive sins. Simply, the power to blackmail. Since priests were successors of Peter, who was supposedly in charge of heaven, guess what? If you displeased a priest, you weren't going to heaven.

Verses 22 and 23 sound like other forgeries in The Gospel that obviously were meant to tie together The Gospel and the Acts of the Apostles. Written by the holy vandals, Acts paints a strange picture of the Holy Ghost, leading later to its becoming part of a trinity.

While we're talking about the people who brutalized the gospel of Luke to tie it to Acts, let's look again at Verse 22 where Jesus supposedly breathed on the disciples, giving them the Holy Ghost (Holy Spirit). Then, look at Acts, Chapter II, Verses 1 to 4, where it is alleged that the disciples were given the Holy Ghost at Pentecost by "cloven tongues like as of fire." That's twice! Even forgers need editors.

OTHER POSSIBLE MOTIVES: Since the forgery in John says the disciples received the Holy Ghost as the result of being breathed upon, as they might have contracted influenza, the holy vandals evidently didn't view receiving the Holy Spirit as a deeply personal experience. And they evidently thought it needed to be DONE twice. They preferred magic tricks to substance. Did they simply not understand, or…?

It is important to understand that the Holy Ghost isn't depicted in The Gospel as the third person of a "trinity." The Holy Ghost wasn't fully defined until centuries later, about the time the church decided

Jesus was a God, not merely the son of God. The word trinity isn't even mentioned in the New Testament.

The Gospel writer John gives us a far different picture of the Holy Ghost and that picture is unlike the supernatural force Paul describes. John doesn't mention any trinity, either.

Instead, in John XIV, Jesus says:

John XIV

15 If ye love me, keep my commandments.

16 And I will pray the Father, and he shall give you another Comforter, that he may abide with you for ever;

17 Even the Spirit of truth, whom the world cannot receive, because it seeth him not, neither knoweth him: but ye know him;

for he dwelleth with you, and shall be in you.

18 I will not leave you comfortless; I will come to you.

Later on in John XIV, Jesus says:

John XIV

26 But the Comforter, which is the Holy Ghost, whom the Father will send in my name, he shall teach you all things, and bring all things to your remembrance, whatsoever I have said unto you.

Jesus said he was going to send the Holy Ghost, or Comforter, or Spirit of Truth to remind us about Jesus' teachings. Does that sound like the forgery about casting out devils, speaking in tongues, handling snakes, etc., that was inserted into Mark? No, the Comforter sounds more like John, or whoever gave us The Gospel. The Spirit of Truth sounds more like The Gospel itself. The Holy Ghost sounds like a combination of the two.

8

SMITING JEWS

Let's look at a simple forgery where the motives easily can be discerned. Consider these verses, which are parallel on the scroll:

Luke V
27 And after these things he went forth and saw a publican named **Levi** sitting at the receipt of Custom; and he said unto him, Follow me.

Mark II
14 And as he passed by he saw **Levi** the son of Alpheus, sitting at the receipt of Custom; and said unto him, Follow me.

Matthew IX
9 And as Jesus passed forth from thence he saw a man, named **Matthew,** sitting at the receipt of Custom; and he saith unto him, Follow me.

The winner is Levi, two to one over Matthew. Applying the pattern of the cross, whose horizontal members are three parallel verses in the synoptics, we have to keep Levi and toss out Matthew.

THE CRIME: Cyril gave Levi the axe and invented Matthew. It is largely because of that forgery that "Matthew" was credited with being the author of the column or gospel that bears his name.

POSSIBLE MOTIVES: Anti-Semitism. The holy vandals' jealousy of the Jews and their religion doubtlessly included the Levites, who were Hebrew clerics. In the Book of Acts, which was manufactured by the Egyptians, a man named Mattatias (Matthew) was chosen by the disciples to replace Judas. He is not, however, mentioned in The Gospel. It is likely that the name was chosen to help tie the so-called gospel of Matthew to Acts.

9

SMITING JESUS

The Alexandrian gang definitely wanted Jesus to be God, so that they could be his earthly representatives, but disliked much of what he preached – like everyone loving his neighbor and priests embracing poverty. So, sometimes they took out their pique on Jesus himself.

The holy vandals, like all Paulists, were very concerned about moral rectitude, and were very certain what moral rectitude was. But it is still hard to believe that they would insert the following two-verse forgery in Mark XIV when Jesus was in the Garden of Gethsemane with 11 disciples:

> **Mark XIV**
> 51 And there followed him a certain young man, having a linen cloth cast about his naked body; and the young man laid hold on him;
> 53 And he left the linen cloth, and fled from them naked.

Those verses have puzzled millions, and they should have. They're gratuitous. They break the crisscross pattern, destroy continuity, and have no parallel in any of the other gospels.

THE CRIME: Making Jesus appear to be homosexual. (Nitpickers, please note: We're saying the forgery and the reason for the forgery were the crime, not Jesus' sexual orientation.)

POSSIBLE MOTIVES: Paul considered homosexuality an abomination, and the largely celibate clergy always has felt self-conscious about it. That is because so many of its members have themselves been homosexuals. So, in their muddled minds – and maybe irritated by the fact that Jesus had so many women friends – they gave him a little slap and, at the same time, made him appear to be more like themselves. Does that make sense?

In any case, the vandals showed over and over that they didn't like much of anything Jesus did or taught. They were more interested in his supernatural powers.

10

DEIFYING MARY

The following three-verse forgery in John XIV is a cynical attempt by the vandals to use the crucifixion of Jesus to further one of their main objectives, the deification of Mary, the mother of Jesus:

John XIV
25 Now there stood by the cross of Jesus his mother, and his mother's sister, Mary the wife of Cleophas, and Mary Magdalene.
26 When Jesus therefore saw his mother and the disciple standing by, whom he loved, he saith unto his mother, Woman behold thy Son!
27 Then saith he to the disciple, Behold thy mother! And from that hour that disciple took her unto his own home.

We know those three verses in John are forgeries when we compare them to single verses in Luke, Mark and Matthew that are the parallels of the 25th verse of John XIV. The parallel verses all say that a number of women, including Mary Magdalene (specifically mentioned in Mark and Matthew), watched the crucifixion "from afar off."

But Mary Magdalene couldn't have stood far away and at the same time stood close to the cross with Mary, the mother of Jesus – close enough to hear his words.

Jesus' mother couldn't have been at two places at once, either, and definitely not at the foot of the cross. What mother could have stood there with the soldiers who drove nails through her son's hands, watching as a spear was thrust into his side and as he suffered and bled? What mother? The vandals didn't understand motherly love. They didn't seem to understand any kind of love.

THE CRIME: In repainting the crucifixion tableau, the vandals put Jesus' mother and the disciple he loved (traditionally John) at the foot of the cross.

POSSIBLE MOTIVE: One of the vandals' main objectives was to deify Mary, so they wrote her a bigger part. They wanted to show that Mary and Jesus were close, while they didn't seem to be at all close. Didn't Jesus ask, "Who are my mother and who are my brothers?" And didn't he say, "A prophet is not without honor save in his own country, and in his own house"?

As to Verses 25, 26 and 27 in John XIV, they're left over when the scroll is restored. Anyway, ask yourself: Would Mary have abandoned her children and gone to live with John? Celibate priests perhaps can be forgiven for not completely understanding love of spouse and children, but Cyril and his associates didn't seem to love anyone, not even Jesus.

11

PROMOTING PRIESTS

Sometimes it is easier to identify vandalism than to guess the motive. Try to figure out a motive for the subtle difference between the following verse in Luke and its parallel verses in Mark and Matthew:

Luke XXIII
46 And when Jesus had cried with a loud voice, he said, Father, into thy hands I commend my spirit: And having said this he gave up the ghost.

Mark XV
34 And at the ninth hour Jesus cried with a loud voice, saying, Eloi, Eloi, lama sabachthani? which is, being interpreted, My God, my God, why hast thou forsaken me?

Matthew XXVII
46 And about the ninth hour Jesus cried with a loud voice, saying, Eli, Eli, lama sabachthani? this is to say, My God, My God, why hast thou forsaken me?

As in the majority of cases, it is Luke that has been tampered with here, omitting God and substituting the word "father."

THE CRIME: In Luke, the vandals' favorite gospel, words are taken out of Jesus' mouth. Instead of asking God why he has been forsaken, as he does in Mark and Matthew, Jesus commends his spirit into the hands of his "father."

POSSIBLE MOTIVES: One can make an educated guess. God is always God, but father also can mean a bishop or priest, and today that altered verse in Luke is used in eliciting deathbed gifts to the church. Jesus warned about calling anyone father. At Matthew XXIII, Verse 9, he says, "And call no man your father upon the earth: for one is your Father, which is in heaven."

12

DEFENDING PETER, DEFENDING PRIESTS

In the King James Version, AFTER Jesus is taken to Pontius Pilate (Matthew XXVII, Verses 3 to 10), Judas returns to the chief priests the thirty pieces of silver with which he had been bribed to betray Jesus. He repents publicly, leaves and hangs himself.

But when the scroll is restored, Verses 3 to 10 appear immediately after the council of chief priests condemns Jesus – BEFORE he is taken to Pontius Pilate, not after.

So what actually happens is that Judas hears the sentence, repents abjectly in front of the chief priests, the disciples and Jesus himself, leaves and hangs himself. Then they bind Jesus and lead him to Pontius Pilate. The vandals wanted to soft-pedal that.

THE CRIME: Moving a whole section of the gospel of Matthew to put the chief priests and Peter in a better light.

POSSIBLE MOTIVES: Having the chief priests and disciples present for Judas' repentence reflected badly on the chief priests and on Peter, who like the vandals themselves, couldn't bring themselves to forgive sinners.

At Matthew XVIII, Verses 21 and 22, Peter asked Jesus, "How oft shall my brother sin against me, and I forgive him? till seven times?" To which Jesus replied, "I say not unto thee, Until seven times: but Until seventy times seven."

Earlier in Matthew, Jesus explained why:

Matthew VI

14 For if ye forgive men their trespasses, your heavenly Father will also forgive you;

15 But if ye forgive not men their trespasses, neither will your Father forgive your trespasses.

If Peter couldn't forgive Judas, then God couldn't forgive Peter, and the vandals wanted to claim to be Peter's successors. That was the same kind of problem they had to overcome when Jesus called Peter Satan.

It is not our purpose to promote the Book of Acts, because it is the biggest forgery of them all, written by some of the same people who vandalized The Gospel. The following passage from Acts, however, is interesting in the way it treats the same incident that is described in The Gospel:

Acts I

And in those days Peter stood up in the midst of the disciples and said,

16 Men and Brethren, this scripture must needs have been fulfilled, which the Holy Ghost by the mouth of David spake concerning Judas.

17 For he was numbered with us, and had obtained part of his ministry.

18 Now this man purchased a field with the reward of iniquity; and falling down headlong, he burst asunder in the midst, and all his bowels gushed out.

19 And it was known unto all dwellers at Jerusalem; insomuch that that field is called in their proper tongue Aceldama, that is to say, The field of Blood.

THE CRIME: Making Judas' death more gruesome. Also having Peter say that Judas kept the bribe money and bought a potter's field for burying strangers. According to Matthew, however, the high priests took back the money but, thinking they couldn't keep it because it was blood money, bought the field.

POSSIBLE MOTIVES: The vandals apparently thought – as they say in Western movies – that "hangin's too good" for Judas. At the same time, they wanted to make the Hebrew chief priests, who were their vocational counterparts, appear to be a little better than they actually were.

13

SMITING LOVE

One of the most difficult things to realize is that although Theophilus, Cyril and associates were all men of the cloth, they actually didn't love Jesus very much, and they especially didn't love Jesus' commandment to "Love thy neighbor." We know the latter because we find them removing or watering down the idea in more than one place.

The following three parallel verses in Luke, Mark and Matthew all originally included "thou shalt love thy neighbor as thyself," but the commandment was removed from both Luke, which the vandals arrogated for their own, and from Mark. Jesus' own commandment, surviving only in Matthew, is boldfaced :

> **Luke XVIII**
> And Jesus said unto him, Why callest thou me good?
> None is good save one, THAT is God.
> Thou knowest the commandments, Do not commit adultery, Do not kill, Do not steal, Do not bear false witness, Honor thy father and thy mother.

Mark X

And Jesus said unto him, Why callest thou me good?
There is none good but one, that is God.
Thou knowest the commandments. Do not commit
adultery, Do not kill, Do not steal, Do not bear false
witness, Defraud not, Honour thy father and mother.

Matthew XIX

And he said unto him, Why callest thou me good?
There is none good but one, that is, God: But if thou
wilt enter into life, keep the commandments.
He saith unto him, Which? Jesus said, Thou shalt do
no murder, Thou shalt not commit adultery, Thou
shalt not steal, Thou shalt not bear false witness, Honor
they father and thy mother; **and thou shalt love thy
neighbor as thyself.**

There is another attack on "love thy neighbor" in the account of
the Last Supper where Jesus says three times: "These things I command
you, that ye love one another." The vandals transposed two of them,
apparently attempting to soft-pedal them.

One of those transposed "love thy neighbor" verses is found at John
XV, Verse 17, where it was parked by the vandals. After that verse is
restored to its original place, before Verse 9 in Chapter XV, the three-
verse paragraph reads smoothly, to wit:

**17 These things I command you, that ye love one
another**

9 As the Father hath loved me, so have I loved you;
continue ye in my love.
10 If ye keep my commandments ye shall abide in my
love; even as I have kept my Father's commandments,
and abide in his love.

THE CRIME: Jesus said "Love thy neighbor," and the vandals edited it out.

POSSIBLE MOTIVES: As everybody knows, Jesus' commandment to "Love thy neighbor" is the most difficult commandment to follow. Following it apparently was impossible for the murderous, misanthropic bunch from Alexandria.

14

'DOCTORING' LUKE

In their efforts to Sanitize Luke, the holy vandals erased four verses. Below, in boldface and contained in brackets [ ], are approximations of the original four verses, extrapolated from the undisturbed formerly parallel verses in Mark and Matthew.

Luke XXII

47 And while he yet spake, behold a multitude, and he that was called Judas, one of the twelve, went before him, and drew near unto Jesus to kiss him.
[**And he that betrayed him had given them a token, saying, Whomsoever I shall kiss, that same is he; take him, and lead him away safely.**
[**And as soon as he was come, he goeth straightway to him, and saith, Master, master, and kissed him.**
[**Then came they and stretched forth their hands, and took him.**]

52 Then Jesus said unto the chief priests and captains of the temple, and the elders, which were come to him, Be

ye come out as against a thief, with swords and staves? When I was daily with you in the temple, ye stretched forth no hands against me; but this is your hour, and the power of darkness.

[And they all forsook him and fled.]

This reconstruction, plus removal of the bogus yarn about Peter wielding a sword (discussed elsewhere) brings this portion of Luke back into alignment with Mark XIV, Verses 43-46, restoring the crisscross pattern.

THE CRIME: Trashing four verses in Luke.

POSSIBLE MOTIVES: The vandals deleted those verses in Luke, the gospel they arrogated to themselves, because they didn't like them so close to a mention of the chief priests. The vandals, of course, were chief priests. Moreover, they didn't like it to be said that ALL of the disciples forsook Jesus, because that would include Peter, whom they had chosen to head their church.

15

SMITING JEWS

We have seen a case where parenthetical tares were sown in Mark and Matthew to encourage violence against the Jews. In John VII, Verses 21 and 22, a parenthetical tare was sown to minimize Moses, the Hebrew lawgiver. It shows that, when it came to the Jews, the holy vandals could be vicious and petty at the same time. Here is how the verses read in the King James Version of the New Testament:

> **John VII**
> Jesus answered and said unto them I have done one work and ye all marvel.
> Moses therefore gave unto you circumcision (**not because it is of Moses, but of the fathers**) and ye on the sabbath day circumcise a man.

As in all cases in The Gospel, wherever words appear in parentheses, they are forgeries. This forgery interrupts the flow of narrative, and its elimination restores that flow. To those who may be tempted to say "So what?" it should be pointed out that circumcision has an important spiritual meaning as well as the physical one.

THE CRIME: Attempting to strip Moses of the credit for circumcision.

POSSIBLE MOTIVES: Anti-Semitism. Downgrading Jews by downgrading the founder of the Hebrew nation.

16

PROMOTING PAUL

Neither Paul's epistles nor The Acts of the Apostles belongs with The Gospel. For all intents and purposes, Paul's letters and Acts constitute the two largest Gospel tares – largest by far.

Suffice it to say that Jesus' teachings and Paul's teachings were diametrically opposed. Consider just the law, faith and salvation.

First, about the law, or Ten Commandments. In Chapter V of Matthew, Jesus says:

Matthew V

17 Think not that I am come to destroy the law, or the prophets: I am not come to destroy, but to fulfill.
18 For verily I say unto you, till heaven and earth pass, one jot or one tittle shall in no wise pass from the law, till all be fulfilled.

In sharp contrast, this is how Paul talks about the law in Galatians III:

Galatians III

24 Wherefore the law was our school master to bring us unto Christ, that we might be justified by faith.

25 But after that faith is come, we are no longer under the schoolmaster.

Then, about salvation. In Matthew VII, Jesus says:

Matthew VII

21 Not every one that saith unto me, Lord, Lord, shall enter into the kingdom of heaven, but he that doeth the will of my father which is in heaven.

In sharp contrast, Paul says in Romans X:

Romans X

13 For whosoever shall call upon the name of the Lord shall be saved.

And never the twain shall meet! A detailed comparison would be a waste of time. Jesus preached the Ten Commandments and good works. Paul preached AGAINST the Ten Commandments and good works. Paul said faith is what's important, and that good works are vanity.

17

PROMOTING PETER

THE CRIME: Another forgery, plus another case of turning a single verse upside down and making two verses out of it.

POSSIBLE MOTIVES: To make Peter, the "patron saint" of the forgers, look good, even superhuman.

You'll remember that the pattern is three verses to a paragraph throughout the gospel of John. Although the following section of John XXI from the King James Version seems to fit the pattern, the boldfaced matter doesn't belong:

> **John XXI**
> 4 But when the morning was now come, Jesus stood on the shore: but the disciples knew not that it was Jesus.
> 5 Then Jesus saith unto them, Children, have ye any meat? They answered him, No.
> 6 And he said unto them, Cast the net on the right side of the ship, and ye shall find. They cast therefore, and now they were not able to draw it for the multitude of fishes.

7 Therefore that disciple whom Jesus loved saith unto Peter, It is the Lord. Now when Simon Peter heard that it was the Lord, he girt his fisher's coat to him, (for he was naked,) and did cast himself into the sea.

8 And the other disciples came in a little ship; (for they were not far from land, but as it were two hundred cubits,) dragging the net with fishes.

9 And as soon as they were come to land, they saw a fire of coals there, and fish laid thereon, and bread.

10 Jesus saith unto them, Bring of the fish which ye have now caught.

11 Simon Peter went up, and drew the net to land full of great fishes, an hundred and fifty and three: and for all there were so many, yet was not the net broken.

12 Jesus saith unto them, Come and dine. And none of the disciples durst ask him, Who art thou? knowing that it was the Lord.

13 Jesus then cometh, and taketh bread, and giveth them, and fish likewise.   (and so forth)

First of all, the parenthetical matter in Verses 7 and 8 is gratuitous nonsense, like most parenthetical matter in The Gospel. It interrupts the narrative's flow and should be thrown out, just as it was thrown in by the forgers.

More important, Verses 8 and 9 originally were a single verse. Two "verses" were created by turning the single verse upside down and dividing it into two, one of the vandals' favorite tricks. To restore it, we have to reverse the process, and this is how the original read:

9 And as soon as they were come to land, they saw a fire of coals there, and fish laid thereon, and bread.

And the other disciples came in a little ship; dragging the net with fishes.

With that restoration, it becomes evident that Verses 7, 10 and 12 in the King James were originally a paragraph. Verse 11 (boldfaced and marked with brackets [ ]) violates the pattern in John of three verses to a paragraph, so it is a forgery and should be removed. This is how it should read, plus Verse 13, which also is authentic:

7 Therefore that disciple whom Jesus loved saith unto Peter, It is the Lord. Now when Simon Peter heard that it was the Lord, he girt his fisher's coat to him, and did cast himself into the sea.

10 Jesus saith unto them, Bring of the fish which ye have now caught.

[11 Simon Peter went up, and drew the net to land full of great fishes, an hundred and fifty and three: and for all there were so many, yet was not the net broken.]

12 Jesus saith unto them, Come and dine. And none of the disciples durst ask him, Who art thou? knowing that it was the Lord.

13 Jesus then cometh, and taketh bread, and giveth them, and fish likewise.

THE CRIME: Embellishing Peter's image.

POSSIBLE MOTIVES: The vandals claimed to be Peter's successors, so they wrote Verse 11 to make him a superman. Verse 6 tells us that the disciples working together couldn't draw in the net. The forgery tells us that Peter DID pull in the net and that it was a wonder it didn't break under the weight of 153 fish.

18

DEIFYING JESUS

As we said before, finding and reversing vandalism in the gospel of John is a bit more difficult than finding and reversing changes made in the snyoptic gospels: Luke, Mark and Matthew.

Although there are some parallel verses in all four gospels, not enough crosses are formed when John is placed side by side with the other three. But in the case of Luke, Mark and Matthew, we know with almost mathematical certainty when a restoration has been made correctly.

We DO, however, know some things about John. The fact that there are any parallel verses at all proves that John belongs with the synoptics. And we know that John was written in a pattern of three verses to a paragraph, which only the author of The Gospel could have conceived. Above all, we can see that John provides the continuity between the restored chapters of the other three; it's the glue that held the original Gospel together.

But how can we tell when the gospel of John is faithful to the original, and when it has been tampered with? With John, because of that gospel's special function, we are forced to follow secondary patterns or clues but, fortunately, the author has used secondary patterns liberally in constructing John, probably more than in any of the others. We know our restoration is correct when we achieve uninterrupted flow of the story.

The best secondary pattern or clue is repeated key words or phrases (the author of The Gospel obviously was influenced by the Hebrew school of repetition). The all-important first 15 verses of John have been reconstructed below. Notice that certain words and phrases (we've boldfaced some of them) are repeated in each paragraph. Compare the King James Version where, in contrast, the key words and phrases are sprinkled like salt and pepper.

The confusion sown in the Egyptian version, which became the basis for the King James and all other modern versions, is undeniable. It is not suprising, however, in light of bloody wars waged by the early church fathers over the very definitions God, Christ, Jesus and Holy Ghost. Many of those on the losing sides of those questions ended up being anathematized, exiled and murdered.

THE CRIME: It's hard to know where to start, but the beginning is the logical place. Starting with "In the beginning…," the vandals scrambled the most important part of the Christian Bible. You should recognize immediately an attempt to make Jesus both God and Creator, to minimize Jesus' human quality and to downgrade Moses, but the worst crime was trying to make Jesus a god. The latter is a crime because it contradicts Jesus. Jesus said plainly that he wasn't God.

POSSIBLE MOTIVES: The holy vandals were small, selfish, mean and stupid men. They so wanted to create a trinity of gods that they were willing to make gods of Jesus and even the Holy Ghost. One suspects that they might have made Jesus' mother a God, as well, but that would have been four so, in the end, they decided to make Mary the Mother of God – sort of an honorary god. Of course, if Mary were to be Mother of God, Jesus would have to be God. How's that for circular thinking?

Why a trinity? An educated guess would be that the holy vandals wanted a trinity to please their constituency. Most true Egyptians, as opposed to Egypt's ruling Greeks, had the trinity of Isis, Osiris and Horus as their heritage and were slow to accept Christianity. A trinity also was acceptable to some of the Christians of Antioch and other points east, whose ancestors worshipped a trinity of the sun god Mithra, the fertility goddess Anita, and the bull-god Haoma. Haoma, by the way, died, rose again and gave his blood to be drunk. Those who drank it supposedly became immortal.

Now, let's take a good look at those first 18 verses of John, as restored. Ideally, the King James Version and the restored version should be placed side-by-side for comparison, but space doesn't allow it. So please compare the restoration below with the first 18 verses in King James. See how repeated key words and phrases (in boldface type) along with the pattern of three verses to a paragraph in John, allow the passage to be reconstructed. Here it is, unscrambled and, as they say, suitable for framing. (Note the smoother flow, the more logical progression and comparative beauty of the restored text.):

John I (restored)

In the beginning was **the Word,** and the Word was with God, and the Word was God; the same was in the beginning with God.

14 And **the word** was made flesh, and dwelt among us, full of **grace and truth.**

16 And of his fullness have all we received; and grace for grace; for the law was given by Moses, but **grace and truth** came by Jesus Christ.

11 He came unto his own, and his own **received him** not.

12 But as many as **received him,** to them gave he power to become sons of God, even to them that believe on his name;

13 Which were born, not of blood, nor of the will of the flesh, nor of the will of man, but of God.

18 No man hath seen God at any time; the only begotten Son, which is in the bosom of the Father, he hath declared him.

10 He was in the world, and the world was **made by him,** and the world knew him not.

3 All things were **made by him;** and without him was not anything made that was made.

4 In him was life and the life was **the light** of men.

9 That was **the true light,** which lighteth every man that cometh into the world.

5 And **the light** shineth in darkness; and the darkness comprehended it not.

6 There was a man sent from God, whose name was John.

8 He was not **that light**, but was sent to bear witness of **that light**

7 The same came for a witness, to bear witness of **the light,** that all men through him might believe.

19

PROMOTING PETER

In telling the story of the Garden of Gethsemane, only one of the three parallel versions was left untouched by the vandals. It's this one in Matthew:

> 31 Then saith Jesus unto them, All ye shall be offended because of me this night; for it is written, I will smite the shepherd, and the sheep of the flock shall be scattered abroad.
> 32 But after I am risen again, I will go before you into Galilee.
> 33 Peter answered and said unto him, Though all men shall be offended because of thee, yet will I never be offended.
> 34 Jesus said unto him, Verily, I say unto thee, that this night, before the cock crow, thou shalt deny me thrice.

Of course, we didn't know at first that the version in Matthew was correct. We only knew for certain after checking it against John's patterns.

In Matthew XXVI, 51, Peter slices off the ear of a servant of the high priest, but John's patterns prove those verses to be bogus, as well as three verses on the same subject in Luke, one in Mark and four in Matthew. We know that because they violate the pattern of two verses to a paragraph in the synoptics, interrupting the pattern of the cross, and three to a paragraph in John.

Since the Alexandrians were building their church and doctrine of apostolic succession on Peter, the original story would not do. Peter had behaved abominably, denying, then abandoning Jesus, just as Jesus said he would.

So in Luke and Mark, the tare sowers make the following changes:

- When Judas and some men come after Jesus in the garden, Peter supposedly tries to protect his master by wielding a sword. It seems highly unlikely, though, that a fisherman from Galilee would even own a sword, let alone use one, or possess the skill to surgically amputate someone's ear. The vandals make Peter sound more like one of Cyril's thugs than a fisherman.

- At Jesus' trial, Peter supposedly stays in the trial room, choosing not to speak up for Jesus because the priests only want false witnesses. But Matthew testifies against Luke and Mark. In Matthew, Peter doesn't hang around. He denies Jesus three times and leaves the palace.

Later, on his way to be crucified, a man named Simon of Cyrene supposedly takes the cross from Jesus and carries it for him.

THE CRIME: Two of the three accounts of events in Gethsemane have been changed by the forgers.

POSSIBLE MOTIVES: To keep Peter from looking bad, because the Alexandrian clergy based their whole claim to legitimacy on being successors to Peter. Notice also that Simon of Cyrene shares the same name as "the just and devout Simeon" who gushed over baby Jesus in

Jerusalem. And since both of those men are the creations of the vandals, is it mere coincidence that they bear the same name as Simon Peter, and that one of them is from Cyrene, a North African neighbor of Egypt? Why not any one of a hundred other names? It may be a coincidence, but this appears to be more subliminal advertising for Peter.

20

PROMOTING PETER

This following appears in the King James Version soon after Peter is called Satan. The vandals stole these two verses from Matthew XXIV, reversed them and plopped them at the end of what is now Matthew XVI:

> **Matthew XVI**
> For the Son of man shall come in the glory of his Father with his angels and then he shall reward every man according to his works.
>
> Verily I say unto you, There be some standing here, which shall not taste of death, till they see the Son of Man coming in his kingdom.

THE CRIME: The two verses in Matthew above were reversed by the vandals and placed elsewhere. Their parallels in both Luke and Mark also were reversed.

POSSIBLE MOTIVES: The vandals wanted to make these verses, which follow shortly after Jesus calls Peter Satan, seem to say that Peter wouldn't taste death until the second coming. The vandals claimed to be Peter's successors.

This is how all three synoptics appeared originally, with the stolen verses (in boldface type) returned, re-reversed and inserted:

Luke	**Mark**	**Matthew**
Luke XXI 33 Heaven and earth shall pass away; but my words shall not pass away.		
	Mark XIII 31 Heaven and earth shall pass away, but my words shall not pass away.	
		Matthew XXIV 35 Heaven and earth shall pass away; but my words shall not pass away.
Luke IX 27 But I tell you of a truth, there be some standing here, which shall not taste of death, till they see the kingdom of God.		
	Mark IX Verily I say unto you, that there be some of them that stand here, which shall not taste of death, till they have seen the kingdom of God come with power	

Matthew XVI
28 Verily I say unto you,
There be some standing
here, which shall not
taste of death, till they
see the Son of man
coming in his kingdom.

26 For whosoever shall be
ashamed of me and of my
words, of him shall the Son
of man be ashamed, when he
shall come in his own glory,
and in his Father's and of the
holy angels.

Mark VIII
38 Whosoever therefore shall be
ashamed of me and my words
in this adulterous and sinful
generation, of him also shall the
Son of man be ashamed when
he cometh in the glory of his
Father, with the holy angels.

27 For the Son of man
shall come in the glory of
his Father with his angels:
and then he shall reward
every man according to
his works.

21

DEFENDING PETER

Whenever there are two strikingly similar verses in one gospel, that means one of them has been removed from another gospel. In this case, there are two parallel verses in Matthew and one in Mark in the King James Version, meaning one of the verses in Matthew was taken from Luke, which has none. Here they are:

Matthew IX

36 But when he saw the multitudes, he was moved with compassion on them, because they fainted, and were scattered abroad, as sheep having no shepherd.

Matthew XIV

14 And Jesus went forth, and saw a great multitude, and was moved with compassion toward them, and he healed their sick.

Mark VI

34 And Jesus, when he came out, saw
much people, and was moved with
compassion toward them, because they
were as sheep not having a shepherd;
and he began to teach them many
things.

Following is the restored sequence in Luke IX. Verse 36 from
Matthew IX in the King James Version (boldfaced) is returned to its
original position between Verses 11 and 12. Get your King James and
compare this restored sequence in Luke with parallel sequences in Mark
VI (Verses 33, 34 and 35) and in Matthew XIV (Verses 13, 14 and 15)
and see how closely they correspond. Comments follow.

Luke IX

10 And the apostles, when they were returned,
told him all they had done. And he took
them, and went aside privately into a desert
place belonging to the city called Bethsaida.
11 And the people, when they knew it,
followed him: and he received them, and
spake unto them of the kingdom of God, and
healed them that had need of healing.

Matthew IX

**36 But when he saw the multitudes, he was
moved with compassion on them, because
they fainted, and were scattered abroad, as
sheep having no shepherd.**

Luke IX

12 And when the day began to wear away,
then came the twelve, and said unto him,
Send the Multitude away, that they may go
into the towns and country round about, and
lodge, and get victuals: for we are here in a
desert place.

POSSIBLE MOTIVES: The holy vandals would do anything to protect Peter's image, because they wanted to claim to be his successors. The multitude was distraught because John the Baptist had just been executed, and was behaving "as sheep having no shepherd." But this desert place belonged to Bethsaida, the home of Peter, so how could it be said that those people didn't have a shepherd? The vandals didn't want anyone saying that in Luke, the gospel they arrogated for their own, so they changed it.

22

PROMOTING PRIESTS

Material enclosed in parentheses is always a forgery, and Verse 2 in the King James Version of John IV is a perfect example. It comes right in the middle of a sentence!

This is how the beginning of John IV appears in King James:

> **John IV**
> When therefore the Lord knew how the Pharisees had heard that Jesus made and baptized more disciples than John
> 2 (Though Jesus himself baptized not, but his disciples)
> 3 He left Judea and departed again into Galilee.

Compare that with how the first verse of John IV – combining King James Verses 1 and 3 – appeared originally:

> **John IV**
> When therefore the Lord knew how the Pharisees had heard that Jesus made and baptized more disciples than John, he left Judea, and departed again into Galilee.

By substituting the single verse for what had appeared to be three verses, continuity is restored, and the pattern of three verses to a paragraph in John is re-established. This, then, is the beginning of John IV, as restored:

John IV
When therefore the Lord knew how the Pharisees had heard that Jesus made and baptized more disciples than John, he left Judea, and departed again into Galilee.
4 And he must needs go through Samaria.
5 Then cometh he to a city of Samaria, which is called Sychar near the parcel of ground that Jacob gave to his son Joseph.

6 Now Jacob's well was there. Jesus, therefore, being wearied with his journey, sat thus on the well: and it was about the sixth hour.

THE CRIME: Taking the credit for baptism away from Jesus.

POSSIBLE MOTIVES: Crediting Peter and the rest of the disciples gave them a head start on their supposed divine mission of converting the entire world through the magic of baptism. The vandals, who claimed to be successors to the disciples, considered baptism their God-given franchise, and decided to cut out Jesus, the middle man.

23

PROMOTING PRIESTS

The vandals, who were priests themselves, so disliked the idea that priests should embrace poverty that they made two additions at the end of Luke XIV to discredit the notion. The additions are in boldface type:

> **Luke XIV**
> 33 So likewise, whosoever he be of you that forsaketh not all that he hath, he cannot be my disciple.
> **34 Salt is good: but if the salt have lost his savour, wherewith shall it be seasoned?**
> **35 It is neither fit for the land, nor yet for the dunghill; but men cast it out. He that hath ears to hear, let him hear.**

THE CRIME: Verse 34, beginning with "Salt is good," is genuine, having parallel verses in another context in both Mark and Matthew, but it was taken out of the same context elsewhere in Luke and dumped here, out of context.

Also, the first sentence in Verse 35, about the dunghill, is a forgery.

The second sentence in 35 ("He that hath ears…") happens to be genuine, but it was moved here from Luke VIII.

POSSIBLE MOTIVES: The vandals so strongly disliked the requirement of poverty that they attempted to water it down in Luke – their favorite gospel – with extra words. Then, they wanted it known that the idea wasn't fit for the dunghill, and so they added what amounts to an exclamation mark ("He that hath ears…") to make sure no one misunderstood.

The preceding is an example of a passage that gains material at the expense of another part of same gospel, or of another gospel. As a result, the meaning of the passage that loses the transferred material also changes. Take, for example, "He that hath ears to hear, let him hear," which was moved from Luke VIII to Luke XIV.

Following is how the passage in Luke VIII reads in the King James Version, showing the spot from which the "ears to hear" sentence was taken:

> 16 No man, when he hath lighted a candle covereth it with a vessel, or putteth it under a bed; but setteth it on a candlestick, that they which enter in may see the light. 17 For nothing is secret, that shall not be made manifest; neither anything hid, that shall not be known and come abroad.

> **(The "ears to hear" sentence originally was here)**

> 18 Take heed therefore how ye hear; for whosoever hath, to him shall be given; and whosoever hath not, from him shall be taken even that which he seemeth to have.

THE CRIME: Stealing from Peter to pay Paul, as they say.

POSSIBLE MOTIVES: This is a case where the vandals killed two birds with one stone. Today, Verse 18, with the "ears to hear" sentence removed, is often construed to mean that whoever is rich should get more goods and money instead of a better understanding of God's Word.

24

SMITING THE GOSPEL, SMITING JOHN

In terms of style, content and beauty, the First Epistle of John closely resembles the "four books" of The Gospel, and now there is further evidence. Although there is nothing to check it against, as in the case of the gospels, which can be checked against each other, the paragraph pattern in the epistle turns out to be the same as in the gospel of John. There are three verses in every paragraph.

The First Epistle of John is the only New Testament book other than the four gospels written in one of the gospel paragraph patterns. Therefore, it is highly likely that John the gospel writer also wrote the First Epistle, and that Cyril stole it at the same time he stole The Gospel – in the year 431 at the Council of Ephesus.

It doesn't take long to spot vandalism in John I. At the beginning of the first chapter is an apparent four-verse paragraph. Since the pattern throughout the book is three verses to a paragraph, that means one verse is a forgery. The second verse is the false one, and it is boldfaced here:

John I
That which was from the beginning, which we have

THE CRISSCROSS DOUBLE-CROSS

heard, which we have seen with our eyes, which we have looked upon, and our hands have handled, of the Word of Life.

2 (For the life was manifested, and we have seen it, and bear witness, and shew unto you that eternal life, which was with the Father, and was manifested unto us;)

3 That which we have seen and heard declare we unto you, that ye also may have fellowship with us; and truly our fellowship is with the Father, and with his Son Jesus Christ.

4 And these things write we unto you, that your joy may be full.

Verse 2 not only interrupts this sequence, but parenthetical material in The Gospel invariably proves to be counterfeit.

THE CRIME: Verse 1 talks about both seeing and handling the Word of Life, which has to mean The Gospel. Inserting Verse 2 obscures the fact that early Christians learned about Jesus through John's Gospel.

POSSIBLE MOTIVES: Promoting the fiction that Jesus was merely an "oral tradition" until Peter, Paul and friends decided to write about him.

25

SMITING JOHN, DEFENDING PETER

Two missing hunks from the cross reveal that two verses have been deleted from the example on the following pages – one in Luke and one in Mark. The reconstructed missing verses are indicated with boldface and brackets [ ].

We also learn, by applying the crisscross template, that Verse 43 of Matthew XXI is either bogus or, if genuine, was transferred from somewhere else. We soon discover that the verse originally came after Verse 32 in the same chapter. The words *"Kingdom of God"* in both the transposed verse and at its original location, help to identify that location, then the cross proves the restoration to be correct.

THE CRIME: Eliminating a verse in each of the three parallel columns – destroying the two apparently to cover up the moving of the third.

POSSIBLE MOTIVES: The vandals didn't like the idea that failing to listen to John would result in losing God's kingdom. Their man, remember, was Peter, and they wanted Peter to have more importance than John.

This was the original, and apparently offending, context of Verse 43:

Matthew XXI

32 For John came unto you in the way of righteousness, and ye believed him not: but the publicans and the harlots believed him; and ye when ye had seen repented not afterward, that ye might believe him.

43 Therefore say I unto you, The Kingdom of God shall be taken from you, and given to a nation bringing forth the fruits thereof.

Following are the parallel passages with restored verses in Mark and Luke and with Verse 43 in Matthew removed and returned to its original place. Note that, in the restoration, the space vacated by Verse 43 is filled by the last half of what is Verse 42 in the King James Version. Verse 42 actually was two verses in the original, not one.

Luke	Mark	Matthew

Luke XX

17 And he beheld them and said, What is this then that is written The stone which the builders rejected, the same is become the head of the corner.

Mark XII

10 And have ye not read this scripture; The stone which the builders rejected is become the head of the corner:

Matthew XXI

42 Jesus saith unto them, Did ye never read the scriptures, The stone which the builders rejected the same is become the head of the corner:

[**This is the Lord's doing,
and it is marvelous in our
eyes.**]

11 This was the
Lord's doing, and it is
marvellous in our eyes?

42 This is the Lord's
doing, and it is
marvellous in our eyes?

18 Whosoever shall fall
upon that stone shall be
broken; but on whomsoever
it shall fall, it will grind him
to powder.

[**Whosoever shall fall
upon that stone shall
be broken; but on
whomsoever it shall fall, it
will grind him to powder.**]

44 And whosoever
shall fall on this stone
shall be broken; but on
whosoever it shall fall,
it will grind him to
powder.

26

SMITING THE GOSPEL, SMITING JOHN

The restored scroll shows us that the original Gospel both started and ended in John, and didn't include the story of Jesus' birth.

Now, consider these three consecutive verses in the final chapter of John:

> **John XXI**
> 20 Then Peter, turning about, seeth the disciple whom Jesus loved following; which also leaned on his breast at supper, and said, Lord, which is he that betrayeth thee?
> **21 Peter seeing him saith unto Jesus, Lord, and what shall this man do?**
> 22 Jesus saith unto him, If I will that he tarry till I come, what is that to thee? follow thou me.

Verse 21, in which Peter asks a second question before Jesus can answer his first question, is an obvious forgery. It is eliminated in the restored scroll both by the pattern of three verses to a paragraph in John and by the repetition of key words.

THE CRIME: Apparently an attempt to put Peter ahead of John by having him discuss John's future with Jesus.

POSSIBLE MOTIVES: Cyril's point man was Peter, not John, whose Gospel Cyril was butchering.

The last tare in The Gospel is the final verse of John:

John XXI

25 And there are also many other things which Jesus did, the which, if they should be written every one, I suppose that even the world itself could not contain the books that should be written. Amen.

Suffice it to say that the world is a large place, which makes the verse a patently ludicrous exaggeration.

THE CRIME: In essence, saying that John's Gospel didn't do Jesus justice.

POSSIBLE MOTIVES: By intimating that many other accounts already had been written, Cyril was seeking to further downgrade The Gospel, just as he started out to do by splitting it into four parts. And he perhaps was trying the justify his plan to attach Paul's letters, Acts and the rest to The Gospel.

27

PROMOTING CONFUSION

Here are a couple of examples of hidden numbers, one showing how they can help to identify and reverse vandalism. The first example involves two verses from Luke in the King James Version :

Luke VI
10 And looking round about upon them all he said unto the man, Stretch forth thy hand. And he did so: and his hand was restored whole as the other.
11 And they were filled with madness; and communed one with another what they might do to Jesus.

In the above case, the numbers of the verses in the King James Version happen to be the same as their hidden numbers. In Verse 10, the fingers of two hands add up to 10. In Verse 11, "one with another" are 11.

In the following example, an abrupt change in subject raises a red flag, and hidden numbers point to a tare:

Matthew XI
And it came to pass, when Jesus had made an end of

commanding his twelve disciples, he departed thence
to teach and to preach in their cities.
2 Now when John had heard in the prison the works
of Christ, he sent two of his disciples.

The word "two" in Verse 2 indicates that it is indeed probably
the second verse in some sequence. But is it this sequence? It doesn't
appear to belong with the first verse, which contains no indication that
it should be in a No. 1 position anywhere. To the contrary, it contains
the words "an end," meaning last, certainly not first.

So we ask, "Are these verses forgeries, or are they genuine and have
been transferred from somewhere else?" We eventually find that Verse
2 originally followed Verses 19 and 20 in Luke III in the King James
Version (which originally made up a single verse that was improperly
divided by Robert Estienne. Verses 19 and 20 obviously are parts of
the same sentence). Following, then, is how Matthew XI, Verse 2
(boldfaced), appears in its proper context in Luke:

Luke III
19 But Herod the tetrarch, being reproved by him for
Herodias, his brother Philip's wife, and for all the evils
which Herod had done, added yet this **above all,** that
he shut up **John in prison.**

Matthew XI
**2 Now when John had heard in prison the works of
Christ, he sent two of his disciples.**
3 And said unto him, Art thou he that should come,
or do we look for another?

These three verses, then, make up the first paragraph in the restored
Chapter III of Luke. You will remember that the first and last paragraphs
of all of the chapters in the synoptics contain three verses. The words
"this above all" in the restored first verse constitute the hidden number

"one." Also note the repeated key words "John in prison" that tie together the reunited elements.

O.K., now where does the "It came to pass…" verse, now in Matthew XI, come from, or is it a forgery? We discover that it isn't a forgery; it was moved from this context in Luke, where it is boldfaced:

Luke XII

31 But rather seek ye the kingdom of God; and all these things shall be added unto you.

32 Fear not, **Little flock,** for it is your Father's good pleasure to give you the kingdom.

Matthew XI

And it came to pass, when Jesus had made an end of commanding his twelve disciples, he departed thence to teach and preach in their cities.

Luke X

13 Woe unto thee Chorazin, woe unto thee Bethsaida, for if the mightly works had been done in Tyre and Sidon, which have been done in you, they had a great while ago repented, sitting in sackcloth and ashes.

14 But it shall be more tolerable for Tyre and Sidon at the judgment than for you.

15 And thou Capernaum which art exalted to heaven, shalt be thrust down to hell.

12 But I say unto you that it shall be more tolerable in that day for Sodom, than for that city.

The above restorations are verified in several ways: by paragraph, verse and crisscross patterns, plus repetition of key words and hidden numbers.

If these aren't proof enough, there is still another clue, the mention of Herod the tetrarch in Verse 1 of the restored Luke III. It's a hidden number. The author of The Gospel sometimes used the names of rulers (who are "above all," and therefore No. 1) to start chapters. Other examples are:

In Verse 1 of Luke II, where it says, "And it came to pass in those days, that there went out a decree from Caesar Augustus..."

In Verse 1 of John III, where it says, "There was a man, named Nicodemus, a ruler of the Jews:"

In Verse 1 of John VI, where it says, "After these things Jesus went over the sea of Galilee, which is the sea of Tiberius."

28

PROMOTING CONFUSION

Usually, when there are only two parallel verses, one is found in Matthew, one in Luke, and none in Mark. But in the following case, there are two PAIRS of parallel verses, but BOTH are found in Luke. It is logical, therefore, to suspect that one pair was removed from Matthew and that their original place can be found. These are the parallels:

Luke XIX

47 And he taught daily in the temple, But the chief priests and the scribes and chief of the people sought to destroy him.

48 And could not find what they might do; for all the people were very attentive to hear him.

and

Luke XXI

37 And in the day time he was teaching in the temple; and at night he went out, and abode in the mount that is called the Mount of Olives.

38 And all the people came early in the morning to him
in the temple for to hear him.

When Verses 37 and 38 are restored to Matthew, they end up parallel
to Verses 47 and 48 in Luke, all at the ends of chapters.

The following similar verses from John are not a parallel, but when
placed after Verse 48, they make what appears in Luke to match more
closely Verses 37 and 38:

John VIII

Jesus went unto the Mount of Olives
2 And early in the morning he came into the temple,
and all the people came unto him; and he sat down
and taught them.

As seen on the restored scroll, this is a good example of John
providing continuity for Luke, Mark and Matthew.

THE CRIME: Same as Tare 27, sowing confusion. This may have
been a plan gone bad, and the vandals may have gone too far to turn
back. And maybe they just didn't care about the damage they'd caused.
They *were* vandals, remember?

POSSIBLE MOTIVES: Who knows what goes on in a truly criminal
mind? An educated guess would be that the vandals so much liked the
idea of Jesus preaching in a temple, as the holy vandals themselves did,
that they supplied *their* gospel of Luke with a second helping taken
from Matthew. It's probably impossible to determine for certain why
they did it, but it should be fixed, too.

29

SMITING THE GOSPEL

This transposition is big, but the motive, again, is not clear-cut. Why don't you take a shot at it?

This time the vandals relocated an entire chapter. They switched what is now Chapter XIV in the King James Version of John from its original location between Chapters XVII and XVIII. One reason we know this is because at the end of Chapter XIV Jesus says, "hereafter I will not talk much with you," and then he proceeds to talk nonstop, including his prayer, through Chapters XV, XVI and XVII.

Chapters XV, XVI and XVII are Jesus' words at the Last Supper, as is Chapter XIV. Another reason we know that Chapter XIV belongs at the end of the Last Supper is because Jesus concludes it by bidding them: "Arise, let us go hence."

It is absurd to imagine that Jesus would deliver that three-chapter monlogue while walking with 11 of his disciples to Gethsemane. To make himself heard, he would have had to yell his words, including the long prayer.

Restored to its original place after Chapter XVII, Chapter XIV naturally segues into Chapter XVIII, which begins: "When Jesus had spoken these words (at the Last Supper), he went forth with his disciples over the brook Cedron, where was a garden, into the which he entered, and his disciples."

30

DEFENDING PRIESTS

Despite their jealousy of the Jews and their religion, when The Gospel put Hebrew chief priests in a bad light, the Egyptian chief priests sometimes came to the defense of their Jewish counterparts. They apparently were afraid someone would get the idea that all chief priests were alike, that is, bad.

The boldfaced Verse 3 in the following paragraph from Mark XIV is a forgery, along with the next six verses, which aren't included here. Notice how continuity has been interrupted between Verse 2 and Verse 3:

> **Mark XIV**
> After two days was the feast of the passover, and of unleavened bread: and the chief priests and the scribes sought how they might take him by craft, and put him to death.
> 2 But, they said, Not on the feast day, lest there be an uproar of the people.
> **3 And being in Bethany in the house of Simon the Leper, as he sat at meat, there came a woman having an alabaster box of ointment of spikenard,**

very precious, and she brake the box, and poured it on his head.

THE CRIME: Removing the offending text that originally followed Verses 1 and 2 and replacing it with a forgery.

POSSIBLE MOTIVES: The Egyptians didn't like the picture of the chief priests and scribes trying to entrap and kill Jesus.

Now, for the sake of clarity, we'll repeat the first two verses of Mark XIV, then we'll replace bogus Verse 3 (actually 3 through 9) with the original verses. The natural inclination is to suspect that the missing original verses were destroyed, but they are found parked in Mark XII, in the King James Version, where they have become Verses 13 through 17. The text originally read like this (restored verses in boldface):

Mark XIV
After two days was the feast of the passover, and of unleavened bread; and the chief priests and the scribes sought how they might take, him by craft, and put him to death.
2 But, they said, Not on the feast day, lest there be an uproar of the people.

Mark XII
13 And they sent unto him certain of the Pharisees and of the Herodians, to catch him in his words.

14 And when they were come they say unto him, Master, we know that thou art true, and carest for no man;
for thou regardest not the person of man; but teachest the way of God in truth; is it lawful to give tribute to Caesar or not? shall we give, or shall we not give? But he, knowing their hypocrisy, said unto them,

Why tempt ye me? Bring me a penny, that I may see it. And they brought it.

16 And he saith unto them, Whose is this image and superscription: and they say unto him, Caesar's. 17 And Jesus answering said unto them, Render unto Caesar the things that are Caesar's and to God the things that are God's.

THE CRIME: Covering up the actual crime committed by the Hebrew chief priests, which was to call in the Pharisees and Herodians, their allies, to trap Jesus. The vandals inserted their forgery to make it appear that the chief priests didn't follow through on their plot.

POSSIBLE MOTIVES: So priests wouldn't have blood on their hands. Later, the Hebrew priests would turn to another ally, Pontius Pilate, to help with their bloody work.

31

DEFENDING PRIESTS

Although it can't be seen except on a scroll, this example happens to be part of the trunk and roots of one of the "trees" mentioned in Part I – in this case, a "sycamine tree," believed to be like mulberry.

As we've said, whenever a chapter in one of the synoptics (Luke, Mark or Matthew) does not begin and end with a paragraph of three verses, we know something is wrong. This two-verse paragraph at the beginning of Luke XII in the King James Version breaks the synoptic pattern:

> **Luke XII**
> In the meantime, when there were gathered together an innumerable multitude of people, insomuch that they trode one upon another, he began to say unto his disciples first of all, Beware ye of the leaven of the Pharisees, which is hypocrisy.
> 2 For there is nothing covered, that shall not be revealed; neither hid, that shall not be known.

Comparing this with the like part of Matthew tells us that there is a verse missing between Verses 1 and 2 in the King James Version, and it turns out to be Verse 40 from Luke VI. So this is how they should line up after Verse 40 (in boldface) is restored to its original place in Luke with the parallel verses in Matthew on the right, after restoration of six verses now improperly located in Luke XVII:

Luke	Matthew
	Luke XVII (restored to Matt.) 5 And the apostles said unto the Lord, increase our faith. 6 And the Lord said, If ye had faith as a grain of mustard seed, ye might say unto this sycamine tree, Be thou plucked up by the root, and be thou planted in the sea; and it would obey you. 7 But which of you, having a servant plowing or feeding cattle, will say to him, by and by, when he is come from the field, Go and sit down to meat? 8 And will not rather say unto him, Make ready wherewith I may sup, and gird thyself, and serve me, till I have eaten and drunken; and afterward thou shall eat and drink? 9 Doth he thank the servant because he did the things that were commanded him? I trow not. 10 Likewise ye, when ye shall have done all those things that were commanded you, say, We are unprofitable **servants:** we have done that which was our duty to do.
(blank)	

Luke XII
In the meantime, when there were gathered together an innumerable multitude of people, insomuch that they trode one upon another, he began to say unto his disciples first of all, Beware ye of the leaven of the Pharisees, which is hypocrisy.

Matthew X

24 The disciple is not above his master, nor the **servant** above his lord.

Luke VI

40 The disciple is not above his master but every one that is perfect shall be as his master.

25 It is enough for the disciple that he be as his master, and the servant as his lord.

2 For there is nothing covered that shall not be revealed; neither hid, that shall not be known.

26 Fear them not therefore; for there is nothing covered that shall not be revealed; and hid, that shall not be known.

3 Therefore whatsoever ye have spoken in darkness shall be heard in the light; and that which ye have spoken in the ear in closets shall be proclaimed upon the housetops.

What I tell you in darkness, that speak ye in light; and what ye hear in the ear, that preach ye upon the housetops.

THE CRIME: Transferring a verse from one chapter of Luke to another. Moving six other verses from Matthew to Luke.

POSSIBLE MOTIVES: To prevent Jesus from calling the Pharisees hypocrites for claiming superiority. The vandals also didn't like it that their followers could be their equals, and they didn't want anyone to be equal to Peter, since they based their own claims of superiority on being Peter's successors.

Since this tree is so tall and bushy, and book pages are so short and narrow, only part of the trunk (the column of Matthew) and the roots (formed by the columns of Luke and Matthew) are shown. On a scroll, with ample room horizontally, two distinct roots of the tree would be separated by white space where the column of Mark normally would be.

White space between tree roots accounts for much of The Gospel where there are no verses in Mark parallel to those in the other synoptics. Unfortunately, as we've said, it's difficult to visualize except on a scroll.

32

SMITING JESUS, SMITING THE JEWS

CRIME A: In one long passage in John, the vandals are completely unmasked. They manage to attack not only Moses and the God of the Jews but, unbelievably, also Jesus.

First of all, in the process of restoring that passage, the following two forgeries in John V are eliminated:

> **John V**
> 34 But I receive not testimony from man
>
> and
>
> 41 I receive not honour from men

(Those false verses are boldfaced and bracketed in the restoration below.)

POSSIBLE MOTIVES: The forgers refused to accept Jesus' word that he was the son of man, and they wanted it to be known that they didn't accept testimony or honor from men. Paul said something similar – that he got his message straight from Jesus (i.e. God, to his thinking), not from men. Again, Paul and the forgers had the same ideas.

CRIME B: In the same passage of John, the vandals attempted to downplay Moses encountering the burning bush ("a burning and shining light") and receiving the Ten Commandments. To fully appreciate the vandals' work, it is necessary to compare the following restoration with the King James Version. Note the missing verses, the transposed verses, the combining of Chapters V and X, and especially where bogus Verses 34 and 41 (boldfaced and marked with brackets [ ]) have been removed.

John V

31 If I bear witness of myself, my witness is not true.

32 There is another that bear witness of me; and I know that the witness which he witnesseth is true.

33 Ye sent unto John, and he bare **witness** unto the Truth.

[34 But I receive not testimony, etc., is here in the KJV]

[35 He was a burning and shining light, etc., is here in the KJV]

36 But I have greater **witness** than that of John: for the works which the Father hath given me to finish, the same works that I do, bear witness of me, that the Father hath sent me.

37 And the Father himself, which hath sent, me, hath born witness of me. Ye have neither heard his voice at any time, nor seen his shape: but these things I say, that ye might be saved:

35 He was a burning and shining light: and ye were willing for a season to rejoice in his light

42 But I know you, that ye have not the love of God in you.

38 And ye have not his word abiding in you: for whom he hath sent, him ye believe not.

39 Search the scriptures: for in them ye think ye have eternal life; and they are they which testify of me.

40 And ye will not come to me, that ye might have life.

[41 I receive not honor, etc., is here in the KJV]

[42 But I know you, that ye have not the love of God, etc. is here in the KJV]

43 I am come in my Father's name, and ye receive me not: if another shall come in his own name, him ye will receive.

44 How can ye believe which receive honour one from another, and seek not honour that cometh from God only?

45 Do not think that I will accuse you to the Father: there is one that accuseth you, even Moses, in whom ye trust.

46 For had ye believed Moses, ye would have believed me: for he wrote of me.

47 But if ye believe not his writings, how shall ye believe my words?

John X

22 And it was at Jerusalem the feast of the dedication, and it was winter.

23 And Jesus walked in the temple in Solomon's porch.

24 Then came the Jews round about him, and said unto

him, How long dost thou make us to doubt? If thou be
the Christ, tell us plainly.

CRIME C: Switching around Verse 42, "But I know you, ye have not
the love of God in you."

POSSIBLE MOTIVES: That was so much on the mark that the
embarrassed vandals tried to soften its effect. The sequence above
shows that they didn't love God, Moses, Jesus or even John the Baptist.

33

PROMOTING PETER, SMITING JEWS

These three accounts can't all be correct:

IN LUKE: First, Peter denies Jesus, then the cock crows, then the trial occurs.

IN MATTHEW: First, the trial occurs, then the cock crows, then Peter goes out and weeps bitterly.

IN JOHN: First, Peter denies Jesus once, then the trial occurs, then Peter denies Jesus twice again.

We can solve the problem by overlaying the crisscross template, but let's see if we can figure out what happened without doing so.

Jesus predicted that Peter would deny him three times before the cock crowed, and everybody knows that the cock crows just before the dawn. And it says in Luke XX, Verse 66, that "as soon as it was day," Jesus was led to trial. Therefore, the correct order of events is: Peter denies Jesus three times, then he goes out and weeps, then the cock crows, then the trial occurs.

The real order of events is embarrassing to Peter and to Cyril and the rest because, instead of testifying on Jesus' behalf, Peter was a coward. He went out and had a good cry.

The vandals tried to fool us into thinking Peter attended the trial. Then, later, they tried to make us believe that the reason Peter didn't testify was because the court was seeking only "false" witnesses. Where it says that, a crisscross comparison shows us that the word "false" was planted by the vandals.

THE CRIME: Transposing verses to make it appear that Peter was at Jesus' trial, when he wasn't.

POSSIBLE MOTIVES: The prime motive, again, is to keep Peter from looking bad. A secondary motive is to denigrate the Jews and their law, the Ten Commandments, by saying Hebrew priests sought "false" witness. One of the Commandments, remember, is "Thou shalt not bear false witness against thy neighbor."

34

SMITING JEWS, PROMOTING PRIESTS

Jesus met a rich man on the way to Jerusalem, and the encounter is described in Luke XIX. Verse 10 is either a forgery or it was taken from somewhere else in The Gospel. This is how the passage reads in the King James Version, with the counterfeit verse in boldface:

> 8 And Zacchaus stood and said unto the Lord, Behold, Lord, the half of my goods I give to the poor; and if I have taken anything from any man by false accusation, I restore him fourfold.
>
> 9 And Jesus said unto him. This day is salvation come to this house, forsomuch as he also is a son of Abraham.
>
> **10 For the son of man is come to seek and save that which was lost.**
>
> 11 And as they heard these things, he added and spake a parable, because he was nigh to Jerusalem, and because they thought that the kingdom of God should immediately appear.

Dropping the inserted verse restores both the continuity and the synoptic pattern of three verses at the start of a chapter and two verses to a paragraph afterward. The paragraph break (blank space) originally came between Verses 9 and 11.

THE CRIME: Adding words to change meaning.

POSSIBLE MOTIVES: Two thousand years later, the effect of this addition may appear to be trivial. This and numerous other changes, however, when added together, amounted to an effective attack on the Jews, their religion and law. The effect, in this case, is to minimize Abraham, the progenitor of the Jewish people.

Although the Zacchaus story doesn't appear in any of the other gospels, a parallel to Luke XIX, Verse 10 (in boldface) appears in the following context in Matthew XVIII:

> **Matthew XVIII**
> 10 Take heed that ye despise not one of these little ones; for I say unto you, That in heaven their angels do always behold the face of my father which is in heaven.
> **11 For the son of man is come to save that which was lost.**

Finding that parallel has led us to discover another bit of vandalism. It turns out that those two verses in Matthew, in turn, belong in Luke, in a discussion about who would become the greatest in the kingdom of God. This time we'll start out with the crime and the motives:

THE CRIME: Multiple transpositions between gospels.

POSSIBLE MOTIVES: The church hierarchy didn't like either the least to be greatest or the greatest to be servants.

Following is a restoration of the section of Luke from which Verses 10 and 11 of the King James Version of Matthew XVIII were taken, and to which Verse 11 of Matthew XXIII has been restored. Including other transposals, it should read:

Luke

Luke IX

46 Then there arose a reasoning among them, which of them should be **greatest.**

47 And Jesus, perceiving the thought of their heart, took a child, and set him by him, and said unto them, Whosoever shall receive this child in my name, receiveth me.

48 And whosoever shall receive me receiveth him that sent me: for he that is least among you all, the same shall be great.

Matthew XXIII

11 But he that is greatest among you, shall be your servant.

Luke XVII

Then said he unto the disciples, It is impossible but that offences will come; but woe unto him through whom they come!

2 It were better for him that a millstone were hanged about his neck, and he cast into the sea, than that he should offend one of these little ones.

Matthew XIII

[Take heed that he dispise not one of these little ones: for I say unto you, That in heaven their angels do always behold the face of my Father which is in heaven.]

Luke XIX

10 For the Son of man is come to seek and to save that which was **lost.**

Luke XV

3 And he spake this parable unto them, saying, What man of you, having an hundred sheep, if he **lose** one of them, doth not leave the ninety and nine in the wilderness, and go after that which is **lost,** until he find it?

5 And when he hath found it, he layeth it on his shoulders, rejoicing.

As you can see in the King James Version, the vandals ran amock after Luke IX, Verse 48. They deleted the verse saying "he that is greatest among you, shall be your servant," then started scattering verses everywhere. In so doing, their particular dislike for Jesus' definition of greatness becomes evident.

One question remains, and that is: What does removing Verse 11 (about the greatest being a servant) do to Matthew XXIII? Well, that verse is actually part of a three-verse tare that is boldfaced in the King James Version shown below. That verse, and Verse 12, were transported there from elsewhere. We can see that Verse 10 is redundant to Verse 8 and, therefore, counterfeit. A two-verse paragraph in Matthew XII, King James Version, belongs in this spot.

Below, you have the King James Version with the three-verse tare in boldface. After that is the restored text with the original two-verse paragraph:

Matthew XXIII
(King James Version before restoration)

8 But be not ye called Rabbi: for one is your master, even Christ; and all ye are brethren.

9 And call no man our father upon earth; for one is your Father, which is in heaven.

10 Neither be ye called masters; for one is your Master even Christ

11 But he that is greatest among you shall be your servant.

12 And whosoever shall exalt himself shall be abased; and he that shall humble himself shall be exalted.

13 But woe unto you, scribes and Pharisees, hypocrites! for ye shut up the kingdom of heaven against men; for ye neither go in yourselves, neither suffer ye them that are entering to go in.

14 Woe unto you, scribes and Pharisees, hypocrites! for ye devour widows houses, and for a pretence make long prayer; therefore ye shall receive the greater damnation.

Matthew XXIII

(Restored)

8 But be not ye called Rabbi: for one is you master, even Christ; and all ye are brethren.

9 And call no man your father on earth; for one is your father, which is in heaven.

Matthew XII

36 But I say unto you, That every idle word that men shall speak, they shall give account thereof in the day of judgment.

37 For by thy words thou shall be justified, and by thy words thou shalt be condemned.

13 But woe unto you, scribes and Pharisees, hypocrites! for ye neither go in yourselves, neither suffer ye them that are entering to go in.

14 Woe unto you, scribes and Pharisees, hypocrites! for ye devour widows' houses, and for a pretence make long prayer; therefore ye shall receive the greater damnation.

35

SMITING JEWS

Let's look at a very serious and very complex example of vandalism. It's a triple switch. The first part involves two misplaced verses – Verses 19 and 20 – plopped into the middle of Luke III. They should be removed. The extra verses are boldfaced and marked with brackets [ ] so that you can see how they interrupt the narrative:

Luke III

16 John answered, saying, unto them all, I indeed baptize you with water; but one mightier than I cometh, the latchet of whose shoes I am not worthy to unloose; he shall baptize you with the Holy Ghost and with fire.
17 Whose fan is in his hand, and he will thoroughly purge his floor, and will gather the wheat into his garner; but the chaff he will burn with fire unquenchable.
18 And many other things in his exhortation preached he unto the people.

[19 But Herod the tetrarch, being reproved by him

for Herodias, his brother Philip's wife, and for all the evils which Herod had done.
[20 Added yet this above all, that he shut up John in prison.]

21 Now when all the people were baptized, it came to pass, that Jesus also being baptized, and praying, the heaven was opened.
22 And the Holy Ghost descended like a dove upon him, and a voice came from the heaven, which said, Thou art my beloved Son; in thee I am well pleased.

Thus, the vandals manage to put John in prison before he finishes baptizing Jesus! Why would they want to do that?

Let's look at the comparable section of Luke III, where the misplaced Verses 19 and 20 came from. Where they came from, two genuine verses, now at 29 and 30 in Luke VII, King James Version, really belong. Verses 18 and 19 belong still somewhere else. See how the boldfaced Verses 29 and 30 restore continuity in the first passage. Also notice the key words that tie the restored text together:

Luke III
16 John answered, saying, unto them all, I indeed baptize you with water; but one mightier than I cometh, the latchet of whose shoes I am not worthy to unloose; he shall baptize you with the Holy Ghost and with fire.

17 Whose fan is in his hand, and he will thoroughly purge his floor, and will gather the wheat into his garner; but the chaff he will burn with fire unquenchable.
And many other things in his exhortation preached he unto the **people.**

Luke VII
29 And all of the people that heard him, and the

publicans, justified God, being baptized with the baptism of John.

30 But the Pharisees and lawyers rejected the counsel of God against themselves, being not baptized of him.

Luke III

21 Now when all the people were **baptized,** it came to pass, that Jesus also being baptized, and praying, the heaven was opened.

22 And the Holy Ghost descended like a dove upon him, and a voice came from the heaven, which said, Thou art my beloved Son; in thee I am well pleased.

Now, you may ask, in what context do you find Verses 29 and 30 and, by moving them, how does that affect the losing text? Let's take a look at the spot in Luke VII, in the King James Version, where they appear. These misplaced verses also are again in boldface type:

Luke VII

28 For I say unto you, among those that are born of women there is not a greater prophet than John the Baptist: but he that is least in the kingdom of God is greater than he.

29 And all the people that heard him, and the publicans, justified God, being baptized with the baptism of John.
30 But the Pharisees and lawyers rejected the counsel of God against themselves, being not baptized by him.

31 And the Lord said Whereunto then shall I liken the men of this generation? and to what are they like?

Now, if Verses 29 and 30 didn't belong in the above passage from Luke VII, what, if anything, did belong? The passage above is restored with two verses now at Luke XVI in the King James Version, where again, they completely interrupt the narrative. The restored Luke VII, with the correct verses in boldface, is as follows:

Luke VII

28 For I say unto you, among those that are born of women there is not a greater prophet than John the Baptist: but he that is least in the kingdom of God is greater than he.

Luke XVI

16 The law and the prophets were until John; since that time the kingdom of God is preached, and every man presseth into it.
17 And it easier for heaven and earth to pass, than one tittle of the law to fail.

31 And the Lord said Whereunto then shall I liken the men of this generation? and to what are they like?

Hopefully, you haven't forgotten the two verses that started this chain – the ones that had Herod sending John to prison before he finished baptizing Jesus. We have come full circle. They are reunited with their companion verses as follows (Notice the repeated phrases in boldface, which provide extra evidence that the restoration is correct):

Luke III

19 But Herod the tetrarch, being reproved by him for Herodias, his brother Philip's wife, and for all the evils which Herod had done,
20 Added yet this above all, that he shut up **John in prison.**

273

Matthew X

12 Now when **John had heard in the prison** of the works of Christ, he sent two of his disciples,
3 And said unto him, Art thou he that should come, or do we look for another?

Now take a deep breath, because there is a little more to this one. The problem becomes apparent when we compare the restored Luke VII with what should be its parallel in Matthew. Next, you will see how the restored version of Luke would match up with the King James Version of Matthew on the scroll (it wouldn't).

Luke (restored)	**Matthew (KJV)**
Luke VII 28 For I say unto you, among those that are born of women there is not a greater prophet than John the Baptist, but he that is least in the kingdom of God is greater than he.	
	Matthew XI 11 Verily I say unto you, Among them that are born of women there hath not risen a greater than John the Baptist notwithstanding he that is least in the kingdom of heaven is greater than he.
Luke XVI 16 The law and the prophets were until John; since that time the kingdom of God is preached, and every man presseth into it.	
	12 And from the days of John the Baptist, until now the kingdom of heaven suffereth violence, and the violent take it by force. 13 For all the prophets and the law prophesied until John.

17 And it easier for heaven and earth to pass, than one tittle of the law to fail.

14 And if ye will receive it, this is Elias which was for to come.

15 He that hath ears to hear, let them hear.

Luke VII
31 And the Lord said Whereunto then shall I liken the men of this generation?

16 But whereunto shall I liken this generation?

Verses 12 and 13 in Chapter XI of the King James Version of Matthew are an example of one of the vandals' favorite tricks: They often turned a verse upside down, then made two verses out of it.

So, in our restoration, we reverse the process. We turn 12 and 13 right-side-up, put 13 ahead of 12, and combine them into one verse, as they originally were.

We know that Verse 14 about Elias in the King James Version of Matthew is a forgery, for the usual reasons. First, it disrupts the continuity of that passage and, second, there is no other place in The Gospel where it might fit. Plus, at John I, Verse 21, the Pharisees ask John the Baptist if he is Elias and he answers, "I am not." Elsewhere we have discussed Verse 15, which happens to be authentic, but belongs somewhere else.

Unfortunately, the vandals threw out a verse to make room for 14 and 15 and, while we can't be sure of its exact wording, we know, by applying the crisscross pattern, that the deleted verse essentially said the same thing as Verse 17 in Luke XVI. So, in restoring Matthew, we duplicate the verse from Luke and insert it into the vacated position in Matthew. Fortunately, text only rarely was thrown away.

THE CRIME: It's another attack on the Hebrew religion, which is crime enough, and The Gospel is left cut up and bleeding.

POSSIBLE MOTIVES: Cyril and the others hated the religion of the Jews, and the law of Moses in particular, since the Egyptians broke the Ten Commandments, for example, by stealing The Gospel (Thou shalt not steal) and killing many Jews and others (Thou shalt not kill).

Finally, you will see how the restored version of Luke matches up with the restored version of Matthew. It finishes our work here.

Luke (restored)	Matthew (restored)

Luke VII

28 For I say unto you, among those that are born of women there is not a greater prophet than John the Baptist, but he that is least in the kingdom of God is greater than he.

Matthew XI

11 Verily I say unto you, Among them that are born of women there hath not risen a greater than John the Baptist notwithstanding he that is least in the kingdom of heaven is greater than he.

Luke XVI

16 The **law** and the prophets were until John; since that time the kingdom of God is preached, and every man presseth into it.

13 For all the prophets and the law prophesied until John: and from the days of John the Baptist until now the kingdom of **heaven** suffereth violence, and the violent take it by force.

17 And it easier for heaven and earth to pass, than one tittle of the law to fail.

THE CRISSCROSS DOUBLE-CROSS

[And it easier for **heaven** and earth to pass, than one tittle of the law to fail.]

Luke VII
31 And the Lord said Where-unto then shall I liken the men of this generation?

16 But whereunto shall I liken this generation?

36

'DOCTORING' LUKE

In this case, there are two formerly parallel verses in Matthew, one in Mark and none in Luke. The two in Matthew appear close together in Chapter XXVI:

> **Matthew XXVI**
> 22 And they were exceeding sorrowful, and began every one of them to say unto him, Lord, is it I?
>
> and
>
> 25 Then Judas, which betrayed him, answered and said, Master, is it I? He said unto him, Thou hast said.

THE CRIME: Moving Verse 25 from Luke to Matthew.

POSSIBLE MOTIVES: The holy vandals were concentrating on re-making the gospel of Luke to better serve their interests. In "their gospel," they evidently didn't like any of the disciples, not even Judas, asking if it would be he who would betray Jesus.

The undisturbed parallel verse in Mark reads thus:

Mark XIV

19 And they began to be sorrowful, and to say unto him one by one, Is it I? and another said, Is it I?

Moving the redundant Verse 25 from Matthew to its original position in Luke restores the synoptic pattern of two verses to a paragraph in Luke, as follows:

Luke

Luke XXII

23 And they began to enquire among themselves, which of them it was that should do this thing.

Matthew XXVI

25 Then Judas, which betrayed him, answered and said, Master, is it I? He said unto him, Thou has said.

This is part of a larger transposition of text in Matthew. First, the vandals took the three verses that originally followed Verse 24 and substituted Verse 25 from Luke. Then, they moved those three verses toward the beginning of that chapter where today they are Verses 14, 1 and 16 in the King James Version. This is the last of the Matthew sequence restored:

Matthew XXVI

22 And they were exceeding sorrowful, and began every one of them to say unto him, Lord, Is it I?

23 And he answered and said, He that dippeth his hand with me in the dish, the same shall betray me.

24 The Son of man goeth as it is written of him: but woe unto that man by whom the Son of man is betrayed!

24 It had been good for that man if he had not been born.

14 Then one of the twelve, called Judas Iscariot, went unto the chief priests, and said unto them, What will ye give me, and I will deliver him unto you?

15 And they covenanted with him for thirty pieces of silver.

16 And from that time he sought opportunity to betray him.

ANOTHER CRIME: The foregoing transposition reverses the sequence of events. In the original Gospel, Jesus first prophesies that Judas will betray him, then Judas leaves to betray him. As a result of the vandalism, it now appears in the King James Version that Jesus is talking about something that already has happened – talking like a historian. But Jesus says clearly that "one of you SHALL betray me."

POSSIBLE MOTIVES: The vandals didn't want Jesus prophesying his betrayal by a disciple.

37

DEFENDING PETER, DEFENDING PRIESTS

We'll try to simplify this one as much as we can. We'll just say that for most of the usual reasons, we know that the boldfaced part of the following passage in the King James Version doesn't belong. The scene is the Garden of Gethsemane:

> **John XVIII**
> 4 Jesus therefore, knowing all things that should come upon him, went forth and said unto them, Whom seek ye?
> 5 They answered him, Jesus of Nazareth. Jesus saith unto them, I am he. **And Judas also, which betrayed him stood with them.**
> 6 As soon then as he had said unto them, I am he, they went backward, and fell to the ground.

Is the sentence about Judas manufactured, or was it brought there from somewhere else? First, let's look at another part of John XVIII after it is restored to its original sequence (Verses 25 and 26 are needed to complete the three-verse paragraph pattern of John). Notice the boldfaced redundancy.

John XVIII

15 And Simon Peter followed Jesus, and so did another disciple: that disciple was known unto the high priest, and went in with Jesus into the palace of the high priest.

16 But Peter stood at the door without. Then went out that other disciple, which was known unto the high priest, and spake unto her that kept the door, and brought in Peter.

16 Then saith the damsel that kept the door unto Peter. Art not thou also one of this man's disciples? He saith, I am not.

18 And the servants and officers stood there, who had made a fire of coals; for it was cold: and they warmed themselves and **Peter stood with them, and warmed himself.**

25 And Peter stood and warmed himself. They said therefore unto him, Art not thou also one of his disciples? He denied it, and said, I am not.

26 One of the servants of the high priest, being his kinsman, whose ear Peter cut off, saith did not I see thee in the garden with him?

27 Peter then denied again: and immediately the cock crew.

Peter's redundant "warmings," of course, is another forgery. The vandals manufactured one to take the place of the words about Judas that they moved to John XVIII, Verse 5, and then they separated Peter's "warmings" so that it would not be noticed that they were redundant. It originally read this way, with the original words restored in boldface (Also, notice the repeated key word "stood," tieing the verses together):

John XVIII

18 And the servants and officers **stood** there, who had made a fire of coals; for it was cold; and they warmed themselves; **and Judas also, which betrayed him, stood with them.**

25 And Simon Peter **stood** and warmed himself. They said therefore unto him, Art not thou also of his disciples: He denied, and said, I am not.

POSSIBLE MOTIVES: The vandals didn't want Peter that closely associated with Judas following the trial. They even may have thought it sounded as though Peter was being asked if he was a disciple of Judas.

It is also interesting to see the context in which Verse 24 originally appeared. Verse 24 was part of a three-verse paragraph with Verse 28, which Robert Estienne mistakenly combined into one. To wit:

John XVIII

24 Now Annas had sent him bound unto **Caiphas,** the high priest.

28 Then led they Jesus from **Caiphas** unto the hall of judgment; and it was early. And they themselves went not into the judgement hall, lest they should be defiled, but that they might eat the passover.

POSSIBLE MOTIVES: Putting the blame for the crucifixion squarely on the shoulders of the high priest Caiphas, instead of on Judas or Pilate, made the holy vandals uncomfortable, since they, too, were priests.

38

DEFENDING PETER

A ttached is a restoration of Jesus' prayer at the Last Supper. In John, again, we must rely mainly on repeated key words and phrases and the pattern of three verses to a paragraph. The vandals started scrambling Jesus' words after Verse 9.

This is how repetitions (boldfaced) helped in the restoration:

- Verse 10, containing the key word **glorified,** is followed by Verse 22, containing the word **glory.**

- Verse 21, containing the key words **thou hast sent me,** is followed by Verse 18, also containing **thou hast sent me.**

- Verse 18, containing the key word **world,** is followed by Verse 14, also containing the word **world.**

- Verses 17 and 19, contain the key words **sanctify** and **truth,** showing they were once together. In this case, they originally were parts of a single verse.

- Verse 16 (below, from the King James Version) is undoubtedly a forgery, since it duplicates the last part of Verse 14, and it should be thrown out:

16 They are not of the world, even as I am not of the world.

Jesus obviously was painfully aware that they WERE INDEED of the world. It's hard to admire sloppy forgery, isn't it?

THE CRIME: Savaging even the prayer of Jesus, and doing it for trivial reasons.

POSSIBLE MOTIVES: To downplay Jesus' apparent concern that the disciples someday could stray from the truth. Jesus was talking about all 12, including Peter, the disciple whom the vandals chose to head their church.

In the following restoration, everything beginning with Verse 9 should be compared with the King James Version:

John XVII
These words spake Jesus, and lifted up his eyes to heaven, and said, Father the hour is come; glorify thy Son that thy Son also may glorify thee:
2 As thou hast given him power over all flesh, that he should give eternal life to as many as thou hast given him.
3 And this is life eternal, that they might know thee the only true God, and Jesus Christ, whom thou hast sent.

4 I have glorified thee on earth: I have finished the work which thou gavest me to do.
5 And now, O Father, glorify thou me with thine own self with the glory which I had with thee before the world was.

6 I have manifested thy name unto the men which thou gavest me out of the world: thine they were, and thou gavest them to me; and they have kept thy word.

7 Now they have known that all things whatsoever thou hast given me are of thee, for I have given unto them the words which thou gavest me.

8 And they have received them, and have known surely that I came out from thee, and they have believed that thou didst send me.

9 I pray for them: I pray not for the world, but for them which **thou hast given me,** for they are thine.

10 And all mine are thine and thine are mine; and I am **glorified** in **them.**

22 And the **glory** which **thou gavest me** I have given **them that** they may be one, even as we are one, I in them, and thou in me, that they may be made perfect in one.

23 And the world may know that thou has sent me, and hast loved them as thou hast loved me.

20 Neither pray I for these alone, but for them also which shall believe on me through their word:

21 That they all may be one; as thou, Father, art in me and I in thee, that they also may be one in us: that the world may believe that **thou hast sent me.**

18 As **thou hast sent me** into the **world,** even so have I also sent them into the world.

14 I have given them thy word; and the **world** hath hated them, because they are not of the world, even as I am not of the world.

15 I pray not that thou shouldest take them out of the world, but that thou shouldest keep them from the evil.

17 **Sanctify** them through thy truth: thy word is **truth;** and for their sakes I **sanctify** myself, that they also might be sanctified through the **truth.**

11 And now I am no more in the world, but these are in the world, and I come to thee. Holy Father, keep through thine own name those whom thou has given me, that they may be one, as we are.

12 While I was with them in the world I kept them in thy name; those that thou gavest me I have kept, and none of them is lost, but the son of perdition; that the scripture might be fulfilled.

13 And now I come to thee; and these things I speak in the world that they might have my joy fulfilled in themselves:

24 Father, I will that they also, whom thou hast given me, be with me where I am: that they may behold my glory, which thou hast given me; for thou lovedest me before the foundation of the world

25 O righteous Father, the world hath not known that thou hast sent me.

26 And I have declared unto them thy name, and will declare it: that the love wherewith thou hast loved me may be in them, and I in them.

39

SMITING THE GOSPEL, PROMOTING PAUL

In Matthew, the Sermon on the Mount takes up 111 verses and three chapters. But in Luke, only 33 verses, or part of one chapter, is devoted to the Sermon on the Mount.

Knowing how the vandals usually operated, one might suspect that they took verses from Luke and transported them to Matthew, but that is not the case this time. Actually, Verses 24 to 34 in Chapter VI of Matthew, contained in the description of the Sermon on the Mount, are the counterparts of Verses 22 to 30 in Chapter XII of Luke. But in Luke, they are far separated from the sermon. What happened?

Interruption of the crisscross pattern shows us that neither passage belongs in the Sermon on the Mount. This is probably a case where the vandals wanted to do so much that they just didn't get all of the loose ends tied up and they settled for changing Luke.

The problem with these parallel verses, in the eyes of the vandals, was that Jesus was telling his disciples what they had to do to get to heaven, and the vandals found some of the things he told them to be distasteful. So, in Matthew, they placed the verses in the Sermon of the Mount, which they hoped would make it sound as though Jesus were addressing his remarks to a multitude, instead of only 12 disciples. That group, of course, included Peter.

But the vandals were more particular with Luke, "their gospel." The parallel sequence in Luke originally began with "and he said unto his disciples" and ended with "Fear not, little flock" showing that he wasn't speaking to the multitude, but to the the "little flock" of Twelve. So the vandals moved those verses from Chapter VI all the way to Chapter XII of Luke, far from the Sermon on the Mount, which is Chapter VI in both Luke and Matthew.

Following are two things contained in Verses 22 to 32 of Luke XII which, since the vandals were trying to water them down, they evidently found to be offensive. These paint an ugly picture of the perpetrators;

Luke XII
22 And he said unto his disciples, Therefore I say unto you, take no thought for your life, what ye shall eat; neither for the body that ye shall put on.

and

Matthew VI
24 No man can serve two masters: for either he will hate the one, and love the other; or else he will hold to the one, and despise the other. Ye cannot serve God and mammon.

Also note the following verse from Chapter VII in Matthew's version of the Sermon on the Mount:

Matthew VII
12 Therefore all things whatsoever ye would that men should do to you, do ye even so to them; for this is the law and the prophets.

However, in our King James Version, the next four verses were taken from Chapter V of Matthew and inserted, to wit:

Matthew V

17 Think not that I am come to destroy the law, or the prophets; I am not come to destroy, but to fulfill.

18 For verily I say unto you, Till heaven and earth pass, one jot or one tittle shall in no wise pass from the law, till all be fulfilled.

19 Whosoever therefore shall break one of these least commandments, and shall teach men so, he shall be called the least in the kingdom of heaven: but whosoever shall do and teach them, the same shall be called great in the kingdom of heaven.

20 For I say unto you, That except your righteousness shall exceed the righteousness of the scribes and Pharisees, ye shall in no case enter into the kingdom of heaven.

Then, after those four misplaced verses are restored to their proper place, and a number of transposed verses returned to their right places, the original narrative picks up with Matthew VII, Verse 21 and continues to the end of the chapter.

THE CRIME: Trying to water down Jesus' teachings, and substitute those of Paul and Cyril.

POSSIBLE MOTIVES: In the end of the Sermon on the Mount, as restored, some form of the verb "do" appears six times. Jesus said to "do" his sayings and to "do" good to others. Paul and Cyril, on the contrary, both claimed that faith – as opposed to "doing" – was the important thing. We know faith was uppermost with Paul, not deeds, since the word faith was used almost 200 times in his 13 epistles.

40

DEFENDING PETER,
DEFENDING PRIESTS

At the end of this example, a section from King James Version and a section from the restored scroll are compared. Ideally, they should be shown side-by-side, but space doesn't allow. The key switch involves verses 63, 64 and 65 of Luke XXII – a three-verse paragraph – shown in boldface.

Of course, we now know that such a three-verse paragraph in the synoptics (Luke, Mark and Matthew) belongs either at the beginning or end of a chapter, all other paragraphs having only two verses. When we return this paragraph to the end of the chapter where it belongs, we can make an educated guess about the motive for moving it up in the narrative. Take a peek at the comparison now, then consider the following:

POSSIBLE MOTIVES: The holy vandals, who wanted to claim to be successors to Peter, preferred to have Peter leave the room before Jesus was slapped in the face. For like reason, they didn't want the high priest to be in the room when it happened. The vandals were high priests, too.

First, Verses 69 and 70 are another example of splitting a verse apart to make two verses, then inverting them. By putting 70 ahead of 69, we see how the verses originally appeared as one, and how they appear, therefore, in the restoration:

Luke XXII

70 Then said they all, Art thou then the Son of God?
and he said unto them, Ye say that I am.
(69) Hereafter shall the Son of man sit on the right hand
of the power of God.

Also, notice that there originally was a verse following Verse 71. The first reason we know that a verse has been deleted is that a single verse doesn't make a paragraph, and there are two verses to a paragraph (no exceptions) in the bodies of the synoptics. Then, by applying the pattern of the cross at that point, we find similar verses in both Mark and Matthew. So, in the restoration, we arbitrarily use the parallel words from Mark (boldfaced and in brackets [ ]). To wit:

Luke XXII

71 And they said, What need we any further witness?
for we ourselves have heard of his own mouth.
[**And they all condemned him to be guilty of death**]

THE CRIME: The vandals made transpositions and a deletion in Luke to make it appear that the high priest and Peter weren't present when the priests condemned Jesus to death and their underlings slapped Jesus. That is inconsistent with the accounts in Mark and Matthew, where the face-slapping occurred in the presence of the high priest and after the trial. So, Mark and Matthew testify against Luke.

POSSIBLE MOTIVES: The vandals went to great pains to make the gospel of Luke "special," because they were using Luke and the Book of Acts as the foundation for their church. Apparently they were sufficiently content with protecting Peter and the high priest in Luke that they allowed the accounts in Mark and Matthew to slide.

Now, let's take a look at the whole picture – first the King James Version, then the restored text – and how continuity is restored:

King James

Luke XXII

61 And the Lord turned, and looked upon Peter. And Peter remembered the word of the Lord, how he had said unto him, Before the cock crow, thou shalt deny me thrice.

62 And Peter went out, and wept bitterly.

63 And the men that held Jesus mocked him and smote him.

64 And when they had blindfolded him, they struck him on the face, and asked him, saying, Prophesy, who is it that smote thee?

65 And many other things blasphemously spake they against him.

66 And as soon as it was day the elders of the people and the chief priest and scribes came together, and led him into their council, saying,

67 Art thou the Christ? tell us. And he said unto them, If I tell you, ye will not believe:

68 And if I also ask you, ye will not answer me, nor let me go.

69 Hereafter shall the Son of man sit on the right hand of the power of God.

70 Then said they all, Art thou then the Son of God? and he said unto them, Ye say that I am.

71 And they said, What need we any further witness? for we ourselves have heard of his own mouth.

Luke XXIII

And the whole multitude of them arose, and led him unto Pilate.

Restored

Luke XXII

61 And the Lord turned, and looked upon Peter. And Peter remembered the word of the Lord, how he had said unto him, Before the cock crow, thou shalt deny me thrice.
62 And Peter went out, and wept bitterly.

66 And as soon as it was day the elders of the people and the chief priest and scribes came together, and led him into their council, saying,
67 Art thou the Christ? tell us. And he said unto them, If I tell you, ye will not answer me, nor let me go.
70 Then said they all, Art thou then the Son of God? and he said unto them, Ye say that I am. 69 Hereafter shall the Son of man sit on the right hand of the power of God.
71 And they said, What need we any further witness? for we ourselves have heard of his own mouth.
[**And they all condemned him to be guilty of death.**]

63 And the men that held Jesus mocked him and smote him.
64 And when they had blindfolded him, they struck him on the face, and asked him, saying, Prophesy, who is it that smote thee?
65 And many other things blasphemously spake they against him.

Luke XXIII

And the whole multitude of them arose, and led him unto Pilate.

41

SMITING LOVE

THE CRIME: In the parable of the Good Samaritan, the vandals first deleted a verse from Luke, then they moved 19 verses from Matthew into Luke. Remember, Luke was the gospel they worked on the hardest to convert to their own uses.

POSSIBLE MOTIVES: Removing verses from Matthew was an effort to water down the first commandment of both Moses and Jesus – to love thy God – and the second commandment of Jesus – to love thy neighbor.

First, the parallel portions of Mark and Matthew. A deleted verse, marked with [ ] was deduced in the process of restoring the crisscross pattern. Verse 31 in Mark was originally two verses.

<table>
<tr><td align="center">Mark
(Restored)</td><td align="center">Matthew
(Restored)</td></tr>
</table>

Mark XII
28 But when the **scribes** had heard that he had put the Sadducees to silence, they were gathered together.

Matthew XXII

34 But when the Pharisees had heard that he had put the Sadducees to silence, they were gathered together.

[Then one of them asked him a question, tempting him, and saying, Master, which is the **first** commandment of all?]

35 Then one of them, which was a **lawyer**, asked him a question, tempting him, and saying, Master, which is the **great** commandment in the **law**?

29 And Jesus answered him, The first of all the commandments is, Hear, O Israel; The Lord our God is one Lord; and thou shalt love the Lord thy God with all thy heart, and with all thy soul, and with all thy mind, and with all thy strength.

36 Jesus said unto him, Thou shalt love the Lord thy God with all thy heart, and with all thy soul, and with all thy mind.

30 This is the **first** commandment.

38 This is the **first** and **great** commandment.

31 And the second is like, namely this, Thou shalt love thy neighbor as thyself.

39 And the second is like unto it, Thou shalt love thy neighbor as thyself.

31 There is none other commandment greater than these.

40 On these two commandments hang all the **law** and the prophets.

(At this point came 19 verses that now appear in Luke in the King James Version, starting with Verse 25 and ending with Verse 27 in Luke X and starting with Verse 45 and ending with Verse 48 in Luke XI. Please refer to them in the KJV.)

Note, too, that for some reason, a verse was removed from between Verses 46 and 47 in the second block of text transferred from Matthew to Luke. It is Verse 52 in King James, shown here, and its return restores the three-verse paragraph with which all synoptic chapters and gospels must end.

> 52 Woe unto you lawyers! for ye have taken away the key of knowledge; ye entered not in yourselves, and them that were entering in ye hindered.

In the restored scroll, there are no parallel verses in Luke. The key words "lawyers" and "law" tie together the material in Matthew and the two blocks of text that were moved to Luke.

42

'DOCTORING' LUKE

In the following example, two 3-verse paragraphs were stolen from the column or gospel of John, where the pattern is three verses to a paragraph, and moved to Luke, where the pattern is two verses to a paragraph. Thus, they are easy to spot.

THE CRIME: Cannibalizing material from the other gospels to "improve" Luke, the gospel that the vandals arrogated to themselves.

POSSIBLE MOTIVES: You can determine for yourself what, if anything, was gained.

Evidence tieing Luke XIII to John II includes the key word **Jerusalem** in Verse 4, Luke XIII and in Verse 23, John II. There also is the phrase *"at the season,"* meaning Passover season, in Verse 1, Luke XIII and *"at the passover"* in Verse 23, John II.

Following is John II after restoration of the two paragraphs (in boldface) that the vandals transferred to Luke. Note that a verse now in John XX in the King James Version and material from John IV also belongs in John II:

John

John II

12 After this he went down to Capernaum, he, his mother, and his brethren, and his disciples.

13 And they continued there not many days.

14 And the Jews' passover was at hand, and Jesus went up to Jerusalem, and found in the temple those that sold oxen and sheep and doves, and the changers of money sitting.

15 And when he had made a scourge of small cords, he drove them all out of the temple, and the sheep, and the oxen: and poured out the changers' money, and overthrew the tables.

16 And said unto them that sold doves, Take these things hence; make not my Father's house an house of merchandise.

17 And his disciples remembered that it was written, The Zeal of thine house hath eaten me up.

Luke XIII

31 The same day came certain of the Pharisees, saying unto him, Get thee out, and depart hence, for Herod will kill thee.

32 And he said unto them, Go ye and tell that fox, Behold, I cast out devils, and I do cures today and tomorrow, and the third day I shall be perfected.

33 Nevertheless, I must walk today, and tomorrow, and the third day following; for it cannot be that a prophet perish out of Jerusalem.

John II

18 Then answered the Jews and said unto him, What sign showest thou unto us, that thou doest these things?

19 And Jesus answered and said unto them, Destroy this temple, and in three days I will raise it up!

20 Then said the Jews, Forty and six years was this temple in building, and wilt thou rear it up in three days?

21 But he spake of the temple of his body.

John XX

9 For as yet they knew not the scriptures that he must rise again from the dead.

John II

22 When therefore he was risen from the dead, his disciples, remembered that he had said this unto them; and they believed the scripture, and the word which Jesus had said.

Luke XIII

There were present at that season some that told him of the Galileans, whose blood Pilate had mingled with their sacrifices.

2 And Jesus answering said unto them, Suppose ye that these Galileans were sinners above all the Galileans, because they suffered such things: I tell you, Nay; but, except ye repent ye shall all likewise perish.

4 Or those eighteen, upon whom the tower in Siloam fell, and slew them, think ye that they were sinners above all men that dwelt in Jerusalem? I tell you, Nay; but, except ye repent, ye shall all likewise perish.

John II

23 Now when he was in **Jerusalem at the passover** in the feast day, many believed in his name, when they saw the miracles which he did.

24 But Jesus did not commit himself unto them, because he knew all men;

25 And needed not that any should testify of man; for he knew what was in man.

John IV

43 Now after two days he departed thence, and went into Galilee.

44 For Jesus himself testified that a prophet hath no honor in his own country.

45 Then when he was come into Galilee, the Galileans received him, having seen all the things that he did at Jerusalem at the feast; for they also went unto the feast.

46 So Jesus came again to Cana of Galilee, where he made the water wine; and there was a certain nobleman, whose son was sick at Capernaum.

47 When he heard that Jesus was come out of Judea into Galilee, he went unto him, and besought him that he would come down, and heal his son; for he was at the point of death. 48 Then said Jesus unto him, Except ye see signs and wonders, ye will not believe.

How do we know that Verses 43 to 48 of John IV belong in John II instead of John IV?

First of all, the reason we know they DON'T belong in John IV is this: The first part of John IV is about Jesus meeting the woman at the well in Samaria. In Verse 43, it says Jesus then left thence (Samaria) and went into Galilee, but then Verse 47 says he left Judea, not Samaria. He had to leave Samaria, not Judea.

One reason we know they DO belong in John II is this: Chapter II takes place in Jerusalem, which is in Judea. So when Jesus leaves there to go someplace else, he departs Judea. In John II, as restored, Jesus says, "Nevertheless I must walk today, and tomorrow, and the day following; for it cannot be that a prophet perish out of Jerusalem."

In other words, he plans to leave Judea in two days. Then, at Verses 43 and 47, restored from Luke, it says he left after two days, and went From Judea into Galilee.

Now, what happens with John XX after Verse 9 is returned to its original position in John II? In addition to moving Verse 9 out of John II, the vandals inserted counterfeit verses in John II – Verses 3, 9, 10, 15 and part of 17. In the following restoration, the false verses are included but are boldfaced and marked with [ ] :

John XX

The first day of the week cometh Mary Magdalene early, while it was yet dark, unto the sepulchre, and seeth the stone taken away from the sepulchre.

2 Then she runneth, and cometh to Simon Peter, and to the other disciple, whom Jesus loved, and saith unto them, They have taken away the Lord out of the sepulchre, and we know not where they have laid him.

[**3 Peter therefore went forth, and that other disciple, and came to the sepulchre.**]

4 So they ran both together: and the other disciple did outrun Peter, and came first to the sepulchre.

5 And he stooping down, saw the linen clothes lying; yet went he not in.

6 Then cometh Simon Peter following him, and went into the sepulchre, and seeth the linen clothes lie.

7 And the napkin, that was about his head, not lying with the linen clothes, but wrapped together in a place by itself.

8 Then went in also that other disciple which came first to the sepulchre, and he saw and believed.

[**9 For as yet they knew not the scripture, that he must rise again from the dead.**]

[**10 Then the disciples went away again unto their own home.**]

11 But Mary stood without at the sepulchre weeping; and as she wept, she stooped down, and looked into the sepulchre.

12 And seeth two angels in white sitting, the one at the head, and the other at the feet, where the body of Jesus had lain.

13 And they said unto her, Woman, why weepest thou? She saith unto them, because they have taken away my Lord, and I know not where they have laid him.

14 And when she had thus said, she turned herself back, and saw Jesus standing, and knew not that it was Jesus.

[**15 Jesus saith unto her, Woman, why weepest thou? whom seeketh thou? She, supposing him to be the gardener, saith unto him, Sir, if thou have borne him hence, tell me where thou has laid him, and I will take him away.**]

16 Jesus saith unto her, Mary! She turned herself, and saith unto him, Rabboni! which is to say Master!

17 Jesus saith unto her, [**Touch me not; for I am not yet ascended to my Father: but**] go to my brethren, and say unto them, I ascend unto my Father, and your Father; and to my God, and our God.

POSSIBLE MOTIVES: To belittle Mary Magdalene. Phony Verses 9 and 10 apparently were designed to separate the disciples, including Peter, from Mary. The part of Verse 17 that is a forgery keeps Mary from contaminating Jesus by touching him. In phony Verse 15, the vandals have Mary mistaking Jesus for the gardener, apparently hoping the reader might believe they were strangers.

Jesus and Mary Magdalene weren't strangers. It would seem that Mary accompanied Jesus and his disciples all through Galilee. Also, in John, it is said that Jesus loved Martha and her sister Mary. In Luke, Mary sat at Jesus' feet and listened to him speak.

As for Verse 3, how small can you get? The vandals evidently thought it important that Peter be the first to start running toward the sepulchre, even though he didn't get there until after "that other disciple," probably John.

43

SMITING JOHN

K ey words betray the forgers right up to the end of the gospel of John, which is also the end of The Gospel of Jesus. The words are in italics.

John XXI

15 So when they had dined, Jesus saith to Simon Peter, Simon, son of Jonas, lovest thou me more than these? He saith unto him, Feed my lambs.

16 He saith to him again the **second** time, Simon, son of Jonas, lovest thou me? He saith unto him, Yea, Lord; thou knowest that I love thee. He saith unto him, Feed my sheep.

17 He saith unto him the **third** time Simon, son of Jonas, lovest thou me? (Peter was grieved because he said to him the third time, Lovest thou me?) And he said unto him, Lord, thou knowest all things; thou knowest that I love thee. Jesus saith unto him, Feed my sheep.

The repeated words and phrases are obvious, but also note that the lambs in Verses 15 and 16 become sheep in Verse 17, indicating time progression and that the phrases "second time" and "third time" in Verses 16 and 17 clearly attach them to 15.

The repeated words show that Cyril did nothing to the paragraph above (Verses 15 through 17) but, in determining that fact, we find another tare in the King James Version. It is Verse 14, the one immediately preceding the paragraph above, which belongs after Verse 23. It reads:

John XXI
14 This is now the third time that Jesus shewed himself to his disciples, after that he was risen from the dead.

Verse 14 belongs in the same paragraph with the elsewhere mentioned Verses 22 and 23, having been moved to make way for the counterfeit Verse 21 ("Peter seeing him saith to Jesus, Lord, and what shall this man do?") referring to, it is commonly believed, John the disciple. The vandals also moved the last two verses of The Gospel to the end of Chapter XX to make way for the hyperbolic counterfeit Verse 25 ("even the world itself could not contain the books that should be written"). The Book of John and, therefore, The Gospel, originally ended beautifully, in this fashion:

22 Jesus saith unto him, If I will that he tarry till I come, what is that to thee? Follow thou me.
23 Then went this saying abroad among the brethren, that that **disciple** should not die; yet Jesus said not unto him, He shall not die; but, if I will that he tarry till I come, what is that to thee?
14 This is now the **third** time that Jesus shewed himself to his **disciples,** after that he was risen from the dead.

24 This is the **disciple** which testifieth of these things, and **wrote** these things, and we know that his testimony is **true.**

John XX

30 And many other signs **truly** did **Jesus** in the presence of his **disciples,** which are not **written** in this book.
31 But these are **written** that ye might believe that **Jesus** is the Christ, the Son of God; and that believing ye might have life through his name.

THE CRIME: Trying to sabotage John by denying him credit for The Gospel.

POSSIBLE MOTIVES: The vandals were grooming Peter for great things and were jealous of John, his relationship with Jesus, and his Gospel. And unlike John, they weren't much interested in Jesus' "sheep."

44

AND THERE ARE MORE

Lest you assume that you've already heard everything, we conclude with a few more tares that will become evident when you see the restored scroll. Some of them are significant and the motives are not difficult to imagine. Others seem less significant, and their motives hazy. But even when the motives are not clearly evil, all tares should be eliminated. They're not from Jesus; they're from Jesus' enemies.

Luke XVI
18 Whosoever putteth away his wife, and marrieth another, committeth adultery; and whosoever marrieth her that is put away from her husband committeth adultery.

Matthew XXVI
53 Thinkest thou that I cannot now pray to my Father, and he shall presently give me more than twelve legions of angels?

Luke XVI

19 So then after the Lord had spoken unto them, he was received up into heaven, and sat on the right hand of God.

Matthew XXVII

51 And, behold, the veil of the temple was rent in twain from the top to the bottom; and the earth did quake, and the rocks rent;
52 And the graves were opened; and many bodies of the saints which slept arose,

Luke XXII

36 Then said he unto them, But now, he that hath a purse, let him take it, and likewise his scrip; and he that hath no sword, let him sell his garment, and buy one.

Luke I

28 And the angel came in unto her, and said, Hail, thou that art highly favoured, the Lord is with thee: blessed art thou among women.

Luke XXIV

44 And he said unto them, These are the words which I spake unto you, while I was yet with you, that all things must be fulfilled, which were written, in the law of Moses, and in the prophets, and in the psalms, concerning me.

Luke XXIV

49 And, behold, I send the promise of my Father upon you: but tarry ye in the city of Jerusalem, until ye be endued with power from on high.

John XVIII

11 Then said Jesus unto Peter, Put up thy sword into the sheath: the cup which my Father hath given me, shall I not drink it?

Luke II

49 And he said unto them, How is it that ye sought me? wist ye not that I must be about my Father's business?

Luke X

16 He that heareth you heareth me; and he that despiseth you despiseth me; and he that despiseth me despiseth him that sent me.

Luke XVII

36 Two men shall be in the field: the one shall be taken, and the other left.
37 And they answered and said unto him. Where Lord? And he said unto them, Wheresoever the body is, thither will the eagles be gathered together.

REALITY CHECK

F or any of you who managed to wade through all of the tedious examples
to the end, we have an admission. We never held out the slightest
hope of swaying more than a few of you, but had to get it off our chest.

Aristotle, who said, "Man, by nature, desires to know," obviously
didn't know many Americans. But could ancient Greeks have been
THAT different?

"Modern" people, from dictators to peasants, fear the truth if it
threatens the status-quo. The first thing any dictator does is close down
the newspapers, because his greatest fear is not external enemies, but
that his own people will find out what's going on. And the peasants,
for reasons known only to God, usually end up siding with the dictator,
blaming the press for stirring up "trouble." What a team!

We're talking here about both world dictators and petty dictators,
including some men of the cloth – book burners at heart – who have
a vested interest in keeping us peasants in the dark.

Aristotle, in his mistaken belief that people desire to know, should
have been a journalist – all journalists believe that – but he would
have been an incompetent psychologist. People don't trust the truth.
It causes them to circle the wagons. They fear the truth. They fear the
mere pursuit of truth. Always have. Always will.

Finally, since we promised, we identify "The Illuminator," who
would have illuminated, had anyone listened. They just didn't know how.

A TRUE GENIUS

*"Is not this the carpenter's son?... Whence then hath
this man all these things?"*
— Neighbors discussing Jesus' credentials

For more than 50 years, Winfred Lycurgus Martindale, the man who
restored The Gospel, was a lawyer. He died in 1989 at the age of 89.

Having spent most of his early years in West Milton, Ohio,
Martindale went on to earn law degrees from The Ohio State University
and to serve as an Army reserve officer in World Wars I and II. He
practiced law in Cleveland and was a U.S. attorney for price control
during the Roosevelt and Truman administrations. He was a friend of
Vice President Henry Wallace and supported him in his campaign for
the U.S. presidency on the Progressive ticket.

Martindale was living in Lakewood, OH, a Cleveland suburb, in
the late 1930s when he found the first clues to restoring The Gospel of
Jesus. It was in West Milton about 30 years later that he completed his
work, having moved there in the early 1950s to take over his father's
law practice. As did his father, he practiced law more than 50 years.

Most people liked the brusque but kindly Martindale, although
they regarded him as more than a little eccentric. He was really far from
eccentric, though, enjoying many ordinary pursuits, such as genealogy,
bowling, collecting postage stamps and occasionally attending church

or a Cincinnati Reds baseball game. More than anything, he loved a good argument, and never admitted defeat.

Like most true geniuses, however, Martindale tended to focus on one matter at a time, ignoring all others, which invited ridicule and caused consternation among family and friends. But it was because of that penetrating focus and a lawyer's sharp eye for detail that he was able to solve the riddle of the tare-sown Gospel.

Twenty-five years ago Martindale self-published a book about his investigations which, frankly, was difficult to read, drew no attention and soon was forgotten. The experience caused him more than once to ruefully acknowledge Jesus' words: "A prophet is not without honour, save in his own country…"

You may recall The Gospel account of the mob at Nazareth, Jesus' hometown, trying to throw him over a cliff.

EDITOR'S NOTE: Like Theophilus and Cyril, Winfred Martindale and Darwin Sator were uncle and nephew collaborators. They often discussed the Bible, history and geograph\y and the problems involved in publishing a scroll. Sator promised his mentor that he never would allow the work he started to die, and this book and forthcoming scroll are in keeping with the promise.

The Crisscross, Double-cross **considerably refines, expands upon, and, in some cases, corrects Martindale's theories about who did what, when, where, why and how (journalism, remember). Martindale's restorations, however, still appear to be flawless and unassailable – a brilliant, unparalleled achievement.**

Asia Minor (modern Turkey)

FAQ

Q. Mr. Sator, people who write about religion are mostly a bunch of wackos. What do you have to say for yourself?

A. Basically, nothing. I wish to tell you only that the New Testament was vandalized. We know who did it, why and how they did it, and how it can be fixed.

***

Q: Why should we care that the New Testament isn't perfect?

A: Because it is far, far from perfect. We should care both because of the sweeping extent of the vandalism, and because it reflects the prejudices and hate of the perpetrators. We're talking here about men rewriting God's instruction manual.

***

Q: What makes you a Bible expert?

A: No one knows everything there is to know about a subject but, say, if you spent 40 years studying and performing brain surgery, you're no doubt a pretty good brain surgeon by now. Having spent 40 years on The Gospel, I'm pretty good at that, too. You see, most people haven't devoted a moment's thought to brain surgery or the Bible's integrity, let alone 40 years. You may say, How about people with *real* religious training? and I have to say *especially* not them. They are trained to preach the Bible, after all, not to wonder if there's anything WRONG with it. They have their job, and I have mine.

314

www.ingramcontent.com/pod-product-compliance
Lightning Source LLC
Chambersburg PA
CBHW032056040426
42335CB00036B/261